To DAD
FROM ROY + MAVIS

XMAS 1977

HAPPY CHRISTMAS.

WILLIE JOHN

Willie John

The Autobiography of
Willie John McBride
as told to
Edmund Van Esbeck

GILL AND MACMILLAN

Gill and Macmillan Ltd
15/17 Eden Quay
Dublin 1
and internationally
through association with the
Macmillan Publishers Group

7171 0803 1

Photograph on back of jacket by courtesy Associated Newspapers Group

Printed and bound in Ireland by
Cahill (1976) Limited, East Wall Road, Dublin 3

Contents

Preface

It is now almost twenty years since I first pulled on that rugby shirt at school. Little did I know what experience lay ahead and how much pleasure I was to achieve from life through chasing that queer shaped bag of wind.

I have had great satisfaction in recalling all the countries and places I've visited; countries and places I had read and learned about at school, yet at that time they seemed so unreal. Nevertheless I feel above all that the thing I treasure most is the multitude of genuine friends I've made over those years whom I know will remain true friends always; people whom I may not see for years, and one day will turn up and be received as when we last met. Then to mention the 'lads' with whom I've had the pleasure of touring with and playing against. These are real men who have come through the thick and thin of International Rugby Football, who did not know what it was like to retreat or to give in, although there were bad days as well as good.

The part of the game that is played after the final whistle also has great memories—although it's best not to recall all of these! Yet I feel a great sadness that the playing side of my game at national level is over and I sorely miss being directly involved in the great fever and atmosphere of Lansdowne Road on the big occasion. However, I feel I've lived a full life and I sincerely hope the younger players coming up, and indeed my own children, get half the fun from life that I have found. Indeed my greatest joy has come from the simpler things.

Many thanks to my mother for a good upbringing and in

7

teaching me to appreciate the true qualities of life; through her I inherit my determination. Also to Penny, my wife, for her encouragement over the years. She certainly knows all about washing dirty togs and spending lonely days and nights with Amanda and Paul while I was on tour.

My words cannot express the help of many friends at Ballymena Rugby Club over the years. It is impossible to mention all the names, but I must record that of Syd Millar, my close friend. Many times we battled together for Ballymena, Ulster, Ireland and the Lions. Then there were great and successful days working with him when he was Coach of Ireland and the Lions in South Africa during 1974.

Finally, my sincere gratitude to Edmund Van Esbeck, who inspired the writing of this book. I look on Ned not only as a friend but also as a sincere rugby correspondent who has the game at heart. His criticism I have always found constructive, fair, and in the interests of better Rugby Football. He brought Lions rugby into most Irish homes from South Africa in 1974, and he also managed to bring a large number of players, including myself, to Church to give thanks after winning the Test series. Thank you, Ned, for your great efforts in the writing of this book, and may our readers have much enjoyment from it.

W. J. McBride
Ballyclare
Co Antrim

1
The Beginning and the End

THERE was a 'hwyl' and the men in scarlet. However I was not unused to either the talents of the Welsh team or the awesome and inspiring sound that comes up from the stands and terraces of the Arms Park Cardiff. Many a visiting team has been caught up in the midst of that atmosphere when the Welsh are engaged in international combat.

The afternoon of 15 March 1975 was such an occasion. It seemed to me that afternoon as if the gods as well as the crowd were on the side of the Welsh. It was my 63rd match for Ireland and we had travelled to Cardiff with something more than hope if something less than total confidence. There followed the most traumatic experience of an international career that begun in unlikely circumstances in the more staid atmosphere of Twickenham fourteen years previously and ended that sunny afternoon in Cardiff when, with what seemed like heaven-sent inspiration, the Welsh tore us apart with a performance that was little if anything short of glorious.

The figure of 63 was to have more significance than the number of occasions I had been privileged to play for my country. We had contained the initial Welsh assaults and the vast reservoir of experience in the Irish side suggested that we would contain the Welsh and hope for the breaks to come. Then things began to go wrong. Tackles were missed and before half-time Gareth Edwards, that prince among scrum-halves, scored a great try. It was the preface to a nightmare as Wales, responding to the frenzied exhortations from the terraces, ran up 32 points without reply from Ireland.

The match was nearing its end and as the Welsh piled up

9

the scores, they seemed to draw added inspiration and renewed vigour from the magnitude of their achievement which must have surprised even them. Five times that afternoon, the Welsh broke our defence and it was after a try midway through the second half, by their prop forward Charlie Faulkner of Pontypool (the club which supplied the entire front row for Wales that day), that I knew in my heart that this was for me the last farewell in the green of Ireland. Faulkner's try, out near the left corner flag, was converted by the brilliant out-half Phil Bennett . . . it was that kind of day. As the ball went over the bar, I looked around me and everywhere dejection was written on the faces of my team-mates. All I saw was sadness. Defeat was written on the faces of players with whom I had known the disappointment that comes with being beaten in an international and the elation that comes from victory. The heads were down, heads that had been held high in places as far apart as Auckland and Johannesburg, players with whom I had been proud to travel the world. Scarcely a word was spoken, yet no message was ever delivered with more startling clarity.

We salvaged but one thing from the wreckage; we scored a try late in the game, injury time, when our number eight Willie Duggan, one of the younger of our players, went through from a line-out and broke what had previously been a defence to compare with the Thin Red Line. Then it was all over and Wales had won by 32 points to 4, their biggest victory for 63 years over Ireland—that figure of 63 again.

It was little consolation to be told by friend and foe alike that Wales would have beaten any team in the world that afternoon. As far as I was concerned they had not beaten any team in the world, they had beaten Ireland. It was not the defeat, but the magnitude of it and even now in the coolness of afterthought, I am still haunted by the 28 points margin that separated us from Wales that afternoon.

We wet the shamrock that night; some say that a few of us did more, we drowned it, they will get no argument from me.

Time can be a great restorative and time in its inevitable

fashion has healed the ache of that afternoon in Cardiff, yet there is no doubt at all that it was a major factor in my decision to retire from the representative scene in which I had participated for over sixteen years.

The idea of retirement had crossed my mind more than once during the 1974-75 season, but after the end of the season, the centenary one for the Irish Rugby Football Union, I made no immediate decision. It was not until the end of August that I eventually came to terms with what was in my heart when I saw that conversion by Phil Bennett the previous March. I wrote to the secretary of the Ulster Branch of the Irish Union, Frank Humphreys, and informed him that I did not wish to be considered for Ulster again. That effectively was the end of the representative road which terminated in the *cul de sac* of the Arms Park in unlikely circumstances. But perhaps that was in itself appropriate for it was against an unlikely background that rugby football for me had started. Certainly 63 caps for Ireland, Lions tours, Test appearances for the Lions and tours to Australia and Argentina with Ireland were more than any man was entitled to expect. For one such as myself, whose introduction to the game had been contrived by others rather than on my own will, it was good fortune beyond the bounds of probability. Rugby had given me a life and taken me to places and into company that was quite outside the environment into which I was born. It had also given me a new name, Willie John McBride.

Rugby traditions run deep in Ireland where fraternity has been almost a password. How else can one explain the fact that so many fathers and sons and brothers have played for the country? For many families it is a way of life. There was no such tradition in my family, who ploughed the red earth among the green hills of Antrim in search of a living, close by the little town of Moneyglass. My parents farmed fewer than 50 acres and had five children to support, a daughter and four sons, of which I was the third, born on 6 June 1940 and christened William James.

Sport was not a coin of high value in the homesteads around Moneyglass. There were other priorities in the struggle to keep the little farmsteads going. Our family in particular had little time for such diversions as my father died when I was four and my mother was left with five children to support, and assistance in the endless chores involved in running a farm, was basic for its and our survival.

Yet it was a happy household. We worked hard, but we enjoyed our humble upbringing. We knew much more about the hide of a cow, however, than we knew about the hide of a football. The pig's bladder was a more familiar sight to me than the one encased in a football. Yet life was not without its moments of gaiety, even if the sporting pursuits of the McBride household were confined to the odd half hour snatched in the afternoons when we laid down the farm tools and stole a few minutes to do what we could with a ball, irrespective of its shape or size. Such liberties usually ended with a reprimand from my mother and the demand to get on with the work on hand. Such places as Lansdowne Road, Ravenhill, Twickenham and Murrayfield might as well have been in outer space for all we knew of them in Moneyglass, which then as now housed a mixed community that knows the value of the good neighbour and the security that comes in a rural Irish parish.

My early education, like that of all my neighbours, was gained in the local primary school. The daily journey to and from the schoolhouse was a round trip of six miles for the McBrides. The three mile walk in the morning was usually prefaced by my efforts to relieve a cow or two of her milk and assorted odd jobs. It was, I suppose, good training for the physical demands that were to come later in life but from my earliest years I needed strength of limb to make my contribution to the everyday running of a farm, a task my mother had to supervise as well as rear and educate her children.

It has often been said that a farmer's work is never really done and even now, far removed as I am from the everyday workers of the land, I still subscribe to that philosophy. Certainly there was always much to be done when we returned from school each afternoon. Cows to be milked, land to be ploughed, crops to be sewn and hay to be saved. The harvest to be won and the elements to be fought, by man and horse, for no such luxuries as tractors were on hand; technology was a word that had not come into the life of the farmer. Yet somehow the battle was always won and if there were setbacks, there were no disasters.

Whatever the needs of the farm, my mother made sure that we went to school each day and the hike had to be performed irrespective of the elements; rain, cold or wind were never acceptable excuses in our house for a day off. Nor were they often offered, for this was one aspect of life in which we knew the score and my mother was referee who played it by the book.

My companion on the daily journey was my brother John and he shared with me the great joy of the first mechanisation that came to our aid and saved us the burden of that six mile trot. Initially the walk was still very much a part of the daily routine, but the labour was less severe when my mother bought a bicycle between us. We got great practice for the relay in the use of the bicycle. We devised a system that enabled John to walk for half a mile and me to cycle, with the process being reversed at the end of each 880 yards, though I was never sure if his measurements were as accurate as they might have been. When I had gone a half mile, I left the bicycle at the side of the road and walked on. He duly collected it and cycled for the next half mile, so the walking distance for both of us was reduced by half.

Later we graduated to a bicycle each and that made life easier in every way and removed at least one subject of argument in our house. With four boisterous boys on hand, noise was one commodity that was never short in our house.

When the time came for me to leave the primary school at eleven years of age, my next assignment was at the Ballymena Academy, a school with a good sporting reputation, though my advent to the ranks of its pupils was not going to add much to its sporting background, nor did it for quite some considerable time.

The trip to Ballymena from Moneyglass entailed a journey of almost an hour and that meant catching the bus at 8.15 each morning and returning home at 4.15 in the afternoon. There was work on the farm to be done before I went and work to be done when I came home. The daily routine did not alter, a quick change of clothes on my arrival each afternoon, out on the farm to milk cows or some other labour, then an evening meal and recourse to the books to do the homework in readiness for the next day at school.

Mine was a very ordinary life certainly by modern day standards when the outlook and demands of youth have changed so much, in many respects I freely admit, for the better. From the time I set foot in Ballymena Academy until I reached my seventeenth birthday, there was little change in the pattern of my life. It was school, farm work, and little else. Yet I cannot recall being in any way unhappy. We had our fun, perhaps simple pleasures, yet we did not question the format of our lives. Maybe we knew no better, perhaps there was an in-built sense of obligation on a farm where there was no man of the house.

It is to my mother's great credit that the farm prospered under her direction. The passage of time and the fact that her sons' limbs grew stronger, doubtless helped in the struggle, but by the time I was seventeen, the demands seemed to grow less. For one thing we had a tractor and if some now say 'big deal', that piece of equipment eased many a burden and was by no means an integral part of all the farms of Ireland in the mid-fifties.

Physically, I was always big for my age and the years of my teens were certainly ones of great development in my height and strength if not, as those who had the terrible job of teaching me at school will doubtless say, in the depth of intellect or my capacity for learning from the text books.

Ballymena Academy was a sports orientated school, but I took no part in the sporting pursuits. I had a general interest in sport, but not a particular leaning towards any one game. If I had a favourite, it was probably athletics. For some strange reason I think I fancied myself as an athlete of some potential, but I was never quite sure in what particular sphere I might perform with a degree of success. At school there was often talk about sport and of course most of the boys engaged in it. Ballymena Academy was, and of course remains, very much a rugby playing school. They had sent out some great players, even if they did not have a good record in the Ulster Schools' Cup.

Being big, I was very often the subject of derogatory remarks about being too soft to play rugby, about which I knew as much as an Eskimo knows about a refrigerator. It was certainly desperation more than conviction that finally introduced me to the oval ball. The various houses in Ballymena Academy are called after hills in Antrim. My house was Slemish more noted for St Patrick's sojourn there than for the sporting exploits or spiritual leanings of those who occupied the house in my time.

I think it was a combination of curiosity and persuasion that eventually introduced me to my first game of rugby. It came about a month before Christmas 1957 in my second last year. Slemish were involved in a house match and I was prevailed upon to lend my weight to their challenge. I was big and looked strong and could be of some asset, if even only as a disruptive force. I shall never forget my first match, more noted for its crudity than its expertise as far as I was concerned. I knew nothing about the laws of rugby and, in fact, had never seen the game played. I remember being put into the second row and picking the ball up after the scrum-half had put it into the scrum. I made a frantic dash up the field before being set upon by about six opponents. I found a grave inconvenience the law that decreed you could only pass the ball back and decided it was a stupid piece of legislation. I violated it a few times on my debut as I did the one current at that time which obliged a player to play the ball with his foot after a tackle.

No rugby career can ever have been conceived in greater ignorance than I displayed that afternoon. Yet we won and I scored a try by some miracle. What is more, I had enjoyed myself, on reflection probably more the chance to exercise my physical strength in man-to-man combat than the specific art of the game.

Walking back from the field to the school, the firsts team coach, Bob Mitchell spoke to me and said that I could be an asset to the school team if I would apply myself to learning the laws and he suggested that I take up the game, especially as my size would be a great help.

I put the proposition to my mother when I went home, followed by a request for the money to buy a pair of football boots. Things were going better on the farm now, which was basically being run by my two older brothers, John and Bertie and I could be spared on the odd afternoon. My mother readily provided the thirty shillings required for the new boots and the pride I had in them has never left me. I remember vividly the rough leather texture with the nailed leather studs and bar of leather running across the instep. They served me well.

I was selected for the school third XV the following week and came through reasonably well, knocking a few opponents out of my way being the major contributon I made. But I was learning and what was more important I was willing to learn.

I cannot have done too badly at any rate for I was promoted to the second XV the following week and to my amazement, within a fortnight, found myself selected on the school first XV. Now I was among the big boys and my shortcomings would be exposed by the experts all round me. But I survived. Bob Mitchell took a particular interest in me and his coaching was a tremendous help. Strength in the scrum and around the field was the greatest contribution I could make yet I remember Bob Mitchell telling me one afternoon that I was not using my weight and height to proper effect. 'You are big and strong, but not nearly hard enough. In fact you are lethargic,' he told me.

My instinctive reaction to that remark was that I would show them whether I was lethargic or not. Now I realise that

Bob was a good psychologist as well as an excellent rugby coach.

The schools' cup opened up new avenues of education for me and Ballymena were progressing nicely in it. We eventually reached the semi-final and were drawn against one of the most famous of rugby academies in Ireland, Royal Belfast Academical Institute, more popularly known as 'Inst'.

This was a country versus city affair and it was to our advantage that the game was played at Ballymena. The traditions attached to the whole match largely escaped me, but I was going to welcome the challenge, even if I approached the task against 'Inst' with some feelings of fear that I might make a fool of myself.

I well remember that the player we feared most on the 'Inst' team was a back called David Hewitt. He was the 'rage' of the schools' game in Ulster at that time and a member of a great Irish rugby family. He was later to be my team-mate on the Irish side and he gave an indication of his promise that day by getting the score late in the game that beat us. We were playing well and level at 3 points all when Hewitt, who had been closely marked all afternoon, got one chance and he took it with the class that even at that young age was in-built. So we were out of the cup. That would be the end of my rugby for the season. But not quite; there was another surprise to come.

To my astonishment, I was selected to play for Ulster Schools against Munster at Ravenhill. This was a league entirely unknown to me and in fact I had never been in Ravenhill in my life, nor indeed had I seen what could be described a first class rugby match.

This time Hewitt was on my side, but in the opposition was a youngster named Tom Kiernan and he kicked the goal that beat us that afternoon when I certainly do not think I distinguished myself. At least one press reporter at the game thought so too, for with a great facility for telling the truth he described my performance thus: 'McBride was the biggest boy on the field, but certainly not the best'. Harsher words have been written about me since.

My height was the deciding factor too in urgings that I might pursue athletics with some profit and it was eventually decided that the pole vault would be the most suitable exercise in which I could indulge. No doubt lifted by the success, such as it was, that had attended my efforts as a rugby player, I trained hard to perfect a technique at the pole vault. Here at least I had one advantage, I had plenty of space in which to practice my art. A wooden rod from the hen house seemed ideal for a pole and a hastily and crudely constructed contraption was used to test what height I could attain. I may have been impressing myself, but certainly not one of my brothers, who though he expressed the opinion that I must be loose in the head to be trying the pole vault, said that he could jump higher than me. I cannot remember whether or not he proved his point, but I made some kind of a hand at it at any rate and won the Ulster Schools' Championship.

The following year, my last at school, I again played rugby, this time no promptings or goading from my class mates was necessary. I do not know whether or not my game took on greater refinement and tactical appreciation, but I again made the Ulster Schools' side. Physical powers are obviously beneficial in the schools' game. It would be a different scene when I went out into club fare, but that was not high on my list of priorities when I finally said goodbye to Ballymena Academy and for me it was back to the farm to earn my daily bread. Despite the degree of success that could be said to have attended my belated schools' rugby career, I think it true to say that, despite the great efforts made by Bob Mitchell and others and the countless hours they put in trying to teach me the basics of rugby, I left Ballymena Academy with rather a loose rugby education.

2
Back to the Land

W H E N I left school, I knew my limitations. I most certainly could not be described as an academic and I very much doubt if anyone who taught me at Ballymena Academy would dispute that personal assessment. I never really gave any specific career very much thought, so I went back to the land to help my two brothers run the farm.

Despite the relative success that I had enjoyed at athletics and rugby, I did not seriously contemplate taking either pursuit seriously and indeed for a while did not play any game. Throwing the discus, the shot and engaging in the pole vault were finished for me now. Physical strength rather than technique had carried me through the athletic sphere at school, perfection in the arts of these field events was outside my compass both in terms of will and facility; the odd game of rugby was a different matter, but I did not seek that either.

I enjoyed the work on the farm with one notable exception —picking potatoes, a task that I heartily detested; I avoided that chore whenever I could, but there was of course no truth at all in the views my brothers sometimes put forward, that I was not a bad hand at avoiding other tasks too!

For almost a year, I stayed on the farm and had a few games with a junior club, Randalstown, after being persuaded to join them by our local bank manager. My introduction to the Randalstown club came in the second XV and I never graduated to the firsts. Our means of travelling to away games was in a milk van and my debut for Randalstown came in Belfast. Most of the team were farmers' sons like myself, and without wishing to diminish their efforts, I was sophisticated by comparison with the approach of most of my team-mates. They lacked finesse but never spirit and I remember that first match well; in many ways it summed up our approach. We were beaten — a matter of little consequence to at least one of my colleagues who spoke for more than himself when he said: 'We might have lost, but we sorted that lot from the town out good and proper'.

With two brothers on the farm there was not really scope for a third and it was suggested that I apply to join the bank. I was accepted, a circumstance that would indicate the executives of the Northern Bank saw more potential in me than I saw in myself at the time. But it was a decision I never regretted.

So now it was effectively farewell to the land; at least I would not have to gather in any more potatoes. Everything has its compensations.

My first appointment was to Ballymoney, a small town more than 20 miles from Ballymena. Rugby was again dismissed from my mind, until once more others took a hand, this time players and officials from the Ballymena club, among them Robin Gregg (a former Irish international and at that time in a realm of rugby to which my humble mind did not aspire), Hugh Allen, Jimmy White and others. I cannot find adequate words to express what all these men and so many others did for me.

The friendly persuasion worked and so I found myself in the Ballymena colours. I was picked for the second XV and we won our first match. I cannot remember that my contribution brought about so happy an outcome, though I must have performed better than I realised for I was immediately promoted to the first XV, but not in the second row. I was picked at number eight and made my entry into senior club rugby against Monkstown at their Sydney Parade ground in Dublin. This time my advent to the upper reaches did not coincide with victory, for Monkstown beat us and handed me a lesson. That was the first time I played with Syd Millar, then an Irish international prop. It was the start of an association that was, I think, mutually beneficial. I learned what physical fitness was all about that afternoon in Dublin and just what it was like to be playing with the big boys. There were times when I felt completely out of my depth, but the encouragement I got from Hugh Allen was a great help. 'Play away and do not worry about making a mistake', he told me and when I got a knock and went down he was quickly at my side saying: 'Get up Willie, don't let them think you are hurt'. A good psychologist as well as a very good player was Hugh.

I was retained on the team, but found training a great hardship. My sole means of conveyance was a bicycle, so training meant thumbing a lift from Ballymoney two evenings a week after work and then thumbing a lift back. I walked many a mile on the road between Ballymena and Ballymoney, day and night in rain or shine.

In those days the banks opened on Saturday mornings, so after finishing work at 12:30, it usually meant a quick dash to get to Ballymena or wherever we were playing in time, and I vividly recall arriving at Ravenhill for an Ulster Senior Cup semi-final with just 10 minutes to spare. I also remember that we lost that particular match. My term of office in the number eight berth for Ballymena was brief, but they did have need of my services in the second row where my limitations of pace and agility were less noticeable and not required in the engine room. The grind of training was still difficult for me; the journey twice weekly to and from Ballymena in the depths of the winter was not exactly the greatest of incentives. Syd Millar had gone on the Lions tour to New Zealand in the summer of 1959 thus becoming the first Ballymena man to do so; the honour was utterly appropriate. He was without question one of the best props in the game at that time and a great clubman.

Things were not going equally well for me however and following a spell of indifferent form, I was dropped from the Ballymena firsts. It was a decision that I felt at the time, but it was one I fully realised to be quite correct. It is often said that disappointment sharpens the senses, and it definitely made me resolve that my stay in the second XV would not be of lengthy duration. I thought a lot about what was wrong with my game and I finally brought the problem down to a lack of total commitment to training.

I did not consciously neglect training, but I think it was a physical no less than a mental factor. My appearance for the Ballymena seconds was, I clearly recall, accompanied by a tremendous determination to prove myself. I played against C.I.Y.M.S. seconds in Belfast and played well. I scored two tries in that game and tries scored by me were rare enough to make them notable in themselves. The club officials were impressed enough to recommend an immediate return to the first team and I was selected in the second row for the senior side the following week. I am happy to say that from that date I have never been dropped from my club's first XV. An incident on the Monday after that match against C.I.Y.M.S. seconds is worth recalling if only to illustrate the attitude in the Ballymena club that I found when first I joined which is maintained to this day. I got a phone call from one of the top officials saying how pleased they were at my performance for the seconds and thanking me for taking my demotion so well. They certainly did not owe me that call for they were quite correct to have dropped me, yet I got a great lift to my morale as a result of such a thoughtful gesture.

I played reasonably well during the season, but any thought of possible representative honours never entered my head. I was therefore very surprised when I was picked for Ulster XV, but I emphasise not *the* Ulster XV. We played against a regimental team from the British Army which was captained by the Scottish international, Mike Campbell-Lamerton, a player unknown to me at that time. Campbell-Lamerton's team had done very well in their Ulster games but we beat them at Ravenhill and it gave me a great deal of satisfaction. Yet greater things were on the horizon although at the time I did not realise it.

I played in the Ulster trial for the first time on 28 September

1960 and was picked for the Possibles. The match immediately ahead was against Lancashire. Syd Millar played in that trial too and when the team to meet Lancashire was announced I found to my surprise that I was picked for Ulster. One is supposed to be able to recollect every detail of the first match for province and country, but I cannot remember a great deal about that game. I know that we won, but I had to have recourse to the record books to discover that it was by the overwhelming margin of 29 points to nil. In retrospect that surprises me for I had always looked back on that game as being a hard match. It probably was too, for me at any rate. I kept my place in the Ulster team for the rest of that season; it was not a particularly successful one for we lost to Connacht, drew with Leinster and beat Munster.

The game from that season which I shall never forget however was against South Africa at Ravenhill in January 1961. Our match against the Springboks came late in their tour and at the time, the Boks were unbeaten. This was a team that represented so very well the great philosophy of successive South African sides, 'subdue and penetrate'. They did just that. But it would be quite wrong to suggest that they relied entirely on forward power, though they had it in abundance in all divisions of the pack that included some of the immortals of South African rugby, including the captain Avril Malan, a magnificent number eight in Doug Hopwood and a second row, or to give it the modern terminology, lock, whom I was to get to know very well indeed in a different sphere 14 years later—Johan Claassen, my immediate opponent that day in Ravenhill. Claassen handed me a few lessons that January afternoon which I never forgot. He seemed to do everything so well and yet was never hurried in his play; everything appeared to be done with a specific purpose in mind, and if not, the benefits from the possession he won were turned to account by the backs. In the back division of that South African team were players of superb class. Keith Oxlee was one of the out-halves in the party, the strong and powerful John Gainsford was one of the centres, they had a wonderful

23

wing in Jan Englebrecht and total competence throughout the side. They beat Ulster by 19 points to 6 and the first half was a real nightmare for us as the Springboks ran up 19 points by half-time. Frik Du Preez was also in that Springboks side and I seem to remember him doing a fair share of the scoring. He was another of the truly great Springboks forwards of the post-war era. He was an outstanding flanker and a great second row.

We did a little better in the second half and managed to score 6 points. It was a good Ulster side liberally sprinkled with international players and some who were later to become internationals, including John Hewitt, David Hewitt, Ken Armstrong (one of the pioneers of organised coaching in Ulster many years later), Andy Mulligan, Ian and Jimmy Dick, Jim Donaldson and of course Syd Millar. Perhaps the best testimony to the Springboks' ability is that they managed to thrash such a team so very thoroughly. Nevertheless, it was some consolation that they had done likewise to just about every provincial team they met on the tour.

That was Ulster's last game of the 1960-61 season, which was just as well, because I might not have been picked again after my joust with Claassen.

Time is a great healer and all things are relative, so I was picked on the Ulster side again in the 1961-62 season for the games against Lancashire and Yorkshire. Early that season I had an experience that was to prove really invaluable and one that gave me an appetite for the top sphere.

An Irish XV was selected to meet a British Combined Services side. I was not in the original selection. But Gerry Culliton of Wanderers, a versatile forward who could play in any position in the pack, cried off the Irish team and I was brought in. This game put me into the best pack of forwards I had yet played with. The team was captained by Ronnie Dawson, who of course had led the Lions to New Zealand in 1959 and was Ireland's captain. The front row was Syd Millar, Dawson and Gordon Wood, all of whom had been to New Zealand. My second row partner was Bill Mulcahy, another

Lion; Tony O'Sullivan, Ronnie Kavanagh and Noel Murphy were in the back row.

In such company I felt like the poor relation, but Wood, never exactly short of a word, put me at my ease. I think he led the pack that particular day, at any rate he gave what might loosely be described as a tactical talk before we went on the field. It went something like this: 'Now there are eight of us forwards and we might, if we feel like it, give the backs the ball now and then. We will scatter their bloody forwards to the four corners of the field and it will be utter devastation and annihilation'. This was the first time I played alongside Bill Mulcahy and it was an education. I adopted a policy of trying to be where he was at all times and his strength in the rucks and mauls and his use of the ball impressed me deeply. We did not scatter their forwards to the four corners of the field, but we did win and I got yet another new name in that game.

Most of the players on our side did not know me very well and I had already been given the name Willie John by this time. Gordon Wood however, obviously got it wrong for during one break from a ruck near their line, I had the ball and suddenly from over my shoulder I heard Gordon shout at me 'Right John Joe, pass it'. I did not pass it, in fact I dropped it, but Gordon forgave me that little indiscretion. The Ulster team did reasonably well that season. We had big wins over Connacht and Munster, but lost to Leinster, and after that game the teams for the final trial were announced. I was delighted to get a place in the Blues (Possibles). My second row partner was Brian O'Halloran of U.C.D. and later of Bective Rangers, while the Whites second row consisted of Bill Mulcahy and my Ballymena team-mate, Ian Dick.

I thought a lot about the way I would approach the task of playing in the final trial; eventually I decided that it was going to be a case of every man for himself and God for us all. Individual performances mattered more this time rather than team performance. I knew it was useless trying to take on Mulcahy, especially in the line-out, so I decided that I would mark Ian Dick. The first half was not particularly good either for the spectators or myself, but we did much better after the interval, yet I did not anticipate being picked for the match against England at Twickenham on 10 February.

That January day of the final trial was a fateful one for me in two respects, for that night I had a date with a girl called Penny Michael. She was the daughter of Harry Michael, honorary medical officer to the Irish team. I have learned since that her father warned her before she went out to meet me, to be careful as she did not 'know anything about this boy McBride'. Well the evening was enjoyable and I was also picked for the Irish side, one of no fewer than nine new caps and the team was greeted with less than enthusiasm by the press or the public at large. The general opinion was that the selectors had gone too far in their desire to infuse new blood into the team. However, for me it was the beginning of an association that was to last longer than I had dreamed possible, while my date with Penny Michael was the start of an association that has brought me abundant happiness, two children, and will I know last a lifetime.

3
One Over the Eight

W H E N I look back now on the preparation by Ireland for that game in 1962 and compare it with the sophisticated methods that were to come during the course of my international career, the contrast is not so much remarkable, as astonishing. We had a brief run out on the day before the game and Bill Mulcahy, the team captain, did as much as anyone could do. But he was the prisoner of the system that obtained at the time. His easy and relaxed manner did much to help all the new boys in the team. It is worth naming them, because some were to leave an imprint on the game and change the course of rugby history, certainly in tactical terms.

The experience in the side was represented in the person of full-back Tom Kiernan, who by now was an established international having made his debut for Ireland in the corresponding game two years previously. Kevin Flynn was one centre and Niall Brophy on the left wing, those two and Kiernan apart, the other four backs were new caps; Larry L'Estrange on the right wing, Ray Hunter in the centre, Gerry Gilpin at out-half and we had a youngster who I think had not yet reached his 18th birthday at scrum-half, Johnny Quirke.

In the pack, there was a strong and tough-looking prop called Ray McLoughlin, also gaining his first cap; Noel Murphy, Syd Millar and Mulcahy were the only forwards who had previously played for Ireland, all three had, of course, also played for the Lions by this time. The hooker was Jimmy Dick, and two of the back row forwards Noel Turley and Mick Hipwell were also new caps.

The England side was a good one by any standards. They

had drawn with Wales at Twickenham three weeks previously and not surprisingly were unchanged. They had Dickie Jeeps and Richard Sharp at half-back, John Willcox at full-back and a hard core of good forwards including Phil Judd, John Currie, Vic Harding, Sam Hodgson and Ronnie Syrett to mention just a few. In the words of Gordon Wood, it was 'utter annihilation' but this time we were on the receiving end.

England destroyed us. The first half had not been too bad; we held them reasonably well and were five points down at the interval. In the second half, they took us apart with Sharp being the prime torturer. He scored a try, kicked a penalty goal and converted a try by another of the England backs. 'It was', said a contemporary report, 'an exhilarating display, even at times brilliant, by England. It was most enjoyable for the spectators who even had visions of a new England after this game'. I need hardly add that the author of those words was an Englishman. It was good to know that some people enjoyed the game, I certainly did not; and as I left the field my only consolation was to have earned a cap for Ireland.

For me, the experience was something completely new in every respect. Not alone was it my first time to play in an international but in fact, it was the first international I had ever had anything to do with. I had never seen a rugby international before I played in one; I had never seen Twickenham before I played there. Trips to Dublin and elsewhere were not part of the itinerary for the people in the Moneyglass area. The youngsters who travel today with parents and friends to Lansdowne Road and the other venues will probably not realise that in those days the majority were less affluent than they are today and the motor car was not part of the standard equipment of many families. Television too was a comparative luxury and indeed had only begun in Ireland around that period, nor did international matches get the blanket coverage they get nowadays in areas where television was established. The radio was the basic means of keeping in touch with happenings in Twickenham, Murrayfield, Cardiff and Dublin and that was as near as I had ever got to an international.

At any rate I must have done fractionally better at Twickenham than I thought for to my surprise, I was again selected for the team against Scotland. The selectors were not now imbued with a similar spirit of adventure to that which had led them to pick nine new caps. It was back to a more conservative approach. Ronnie Dawson was recalled as hooker and Gerry Culliton came into the back row; Gilpin was switched to full-back in place of Kiernan and Gerry Hardy, of Bective Rangers, later to die a very young man in tragic circumstances, was at out-half. Dave Hewitt was recalled in the centre and Ray Hunter was on the wing. Dick, Murphy and Turley were gone from the pack; Kiernan and L'Estrange, were gone from a reshuffled back line.

If things were bad at Twickenham, worse was to follow against Scotland who beat us by 20 points to 6. Now the axe would fall in a big way again. Once more I have recourse to the press to explain the general feeling that prevailed at the time. 'Against England', went one article, 'the Irish selectors called in nine new caps; they could be said to have gone one over the eight. Against Scotland, they provided an alleged remedy that could be described as being too little too late. Where does Irish rugby turn now? Backwards at an alarming rate if the present trend is continued. One thing is sure, some of the youngsters called in this season are not the answer and I cannot see many if any of them having extended international careers'. The author of that opinion is still around but I will not name him to spare his blushes, although he did have some valid points. However as is often the case, his condemnation was too severe and his judgement too hasty.

After the game against England, I felt as if I was in an unreal world. The stands seemed to crowd in on me as I walked off the field. It was the first time I had ever been conscious of a crowd. Looking back now, in many ways I seemed to have been in a kind of vacuum. But bad as I felt after Twickenham, I felt devastated after the game against Scotland. This was a real let down in front of the Irish supporters. I remember talking to Bill Mulcahy after the game and asking him what was wrong. I badly wanted to win for Ireland and for myself. Mulcahy's build-up for those two games had been good, but in retrospect, we lacked belief in ourselves. We would make silly mistakes and concede scores. I think too at at the time we did not have players in depth as good as the opposition. Such circumstances were often to obtain in a later era, but keen study of our strengths and our opponents' weakness and a better tactical approach went a long way towards cutting the odds against us, especially as spirit and character have always been an integral part of the Irish make-up.

The question of approach, preparation and strategy involved in international rugby are subjects that I will deal with later and if such matters were exercising the minds of the more forward thinking of rugby players and administrators in the early 1960's, there were far too many in places of power who did not want the old order to change. They wanted Ireland to win, but were not prepared to make decisions that would help towards that goal. Perhaps it was fear that they would lose their power; I certainly believe that such an attitude predominated over what too often was used as an excuse for doing nothing, the possible violation of the amateur principle, and what some like to refer to as the ethos of the game. Ronnie Dawson, during his term as Irish captain just prior to my advent to the Irish side, saw what was required even at that early stage, but his was a voice crying in the wilderness.

Ireland's match against Wales in 1962 was postponed because of an outbreak of smallpox in a Welsh village, so the final game of the season was against France in Paris. I was selected once more but again we lost the game, by 11 points to nil. We were in trouble before the game started as Tom Kiernan, Niall Brophy and Mick Hipwell were all ruled out because of injury. Kiernan in fact had been selected in the centre. Ronnie Kavanagh was recalled to the side and Jimmy Kelly, a fine scrum-half from U.C.D., made his debut for Ireland. Bill Mulcahy played on the flank in that game, but I remember it for a very different reason, an injury that caused me much pain and no little inconvenience.

30

We were doing reasonably well in the game and I broke from a maul with the ball. I made some ground and passed the ball inside to a team-mate, I think it was Ronnie Kavanagh. Just after I made the pass, I got a tremendous kick just above an ankle; unfortunately I cannot escape the conclusion that the kick was no accident. I went down immediately, and Mulcahy, a doctor, had a look at the leg. I was taken off, but had the injury strapped and went back on the field. In those days there were no such things as substitutes or to give them the title so beloved of administrators, 'replacements'. I was silly to go back on the field, but it was either that or Ireland playing on with 14 men and we had enough problems with 15. I knew something had gone for I could feel a sensation that seemed like two bones rubbing together. My contribution before the injury was not of great moment, after the kick on the leg, I was a passenger. I got down in the scrum, but just hobbled around the field from scrum to lineout. We lost the game heavily and I was taken to hospital. X-ray revealed two broken bones, so my leg was put in plaster. It was a sad end to the international season for me. Yet I had survived in the team and that was more than I had expected after successive games that meant defeat for Ireland.

That kick at Colombes Stadium in Paris inflicted on me the only really serious injury I have had in my career, yet incredibly it did not prevent me gaining an honour that I could not have seriously contemplated.

The Lions were due to go to South Africa that summer and there was the usual speculation about the composition of the team. Very few of the critics mentioned my name as a possible so when the team was announced they were surprised to find McBride in the squad. They were not as surprised as I. In any case with my leg in plaster, the odds against my going to South Africa looked long.

The party was due to fly out about the middle of May and the first game was in Rhodesia. The tour captain was the great Scots winger Arthur Smith; Commander Brian Vaughan, the old England international was named as manager, while

Harry McKibbin, who had played for Ireland and the Lions before the outbreak of war in 1939 and now a much respected official, was assistant manager. There were nine players from Wales, eight from England, seven from Ireland and six from Scotland.

4

A Wounded Lion

THREE days before the Lions party assembled at Eastbourne for pre-tour training, I had the plaster removed from my leg. There was, as one would expect, a considerable amount of muscle wastage and when I travelled to Eastbourne, I did so in grave doubt that I would be making the trip to South Africa.

I was examined by a doctor and was surprised and delighted when he said I could make the trip. He told me I would not be able to play for about four weeks, but after that everything should be all right. I doubt if there is even the remotest possibility that such a position would be accepted today, or that a player suffering from a similar type of injury would be selected in the circumstances that obtain now; there is simply no chance he would be allowed to travel.

I remember getting on the plane at London Airport and being just about able to put the foot under me. When I was selected, I spoke to players such as Bill Mulcahy, Ronnie Dawson and a few other experienced Lions and they told me to go out and learn, and do my best. I knew I was green in the ways of top class rugby; physical strength and a great willingness to learn were my only attributes.

There was a lot of strength and a lot of class in the squad and the first match got the tour off to a fine start with Rhodesia being defeated easily in Bulawayo. Yet from the outset, injuries caused problems and that situation continued right to the end of the tour. Sam Hodgson broke a leg in the first match and his role for the remainder of the tour was that of a spectator. The contrast here also is sharp with modern

33

times for now he would be sent home. There is nothing worse on a tour than injury. Day after day I trained, knowing that I had no hope of playing in a game. The leg was getting stronger, there was plenty of encouragement from the management and players, yet I was beginning to despair. I was never unhappier in my life than when that tour was about a month old. I had never been away from home; the whole South African scene was completely alien to me. Then came an added complication with a swelling around my Achilles tendon. This was caused by pressure, so my hoped for debut was delayed yet again.

The Lions had now played five matches and were still unbeaten. I was eventually selected to play in the sixth game of the tour, against South West Africa at Windhoek. The capital of what is now known as Namibia, Windhoek is of course at altitude. I remember the shock I got when I saw the pitch, which seemed covered only here and there by grass. It had been heavily watered to keep down the dust and after 15 minutes of that game I was sure I was about to go to the angels. I was not match fit, the thin air was killing me and I could not breathe properly. I found then and subsequently that games against South West Africa are never easy. That afternoon, we were down 6-3 at half-time, but in the second half, the Lions scored 11 points and so won by 14-6 preserving their unbeaten record. Such a record was not to stand for long.

Our next match was against Northern Transvaal at Loftus Versfeld, Pretoria. I do not know anywhere in South Africa where the spirit of the Boers is exemplified quite like the region in and around Pretoria. One is always conscious of the feeling that here the spectators see a game against the Lions as a continuation of a glorious struggle started on other fields and in spheres other than rugby. I don't make this observation altogether in terms of criticism, but nationalism can at times cloud issues in sport. National pride is something that has sustained the Irish since the beginning of time, but sport must never be used as a vehicle for an extension of outside issues. What is more important of course is the converse of that attitude, defeat must not be taken as a blow to a country politically or socially. I think that some at least in South Africa have their priorities wrong in this respect. Being beaten on a rugby field is not a national disaster.

The Northern Transvaal team that afternoon in 1962 certainly played with a commitment that was highly commendable, but with an attitude that was not. It was an unsavoury match that did nothing to improve the image of rugby football nor, in my opinion, enhance the prestige of a region that has given so much to the game.

Richard Sharp sustained a broken cheek bone in that game to add to other injury problems and these were immense, for after only the fourth game of the tour, the Lions had no fewer than 10 players under treatment. The injury sustained by Sharp was quite unnecessary and was the consequence of an approach by at least one South African player that had more than just a ring of fanaticism about it. The Lions lost the game by 14 points to 6 and I could have no complaint that the better team won. However, the methods used by Northern Transvaal took from the merit of their victory over a side reduced to 14 men after only five minutes—the time it took to put Sharp out of the match.

The next game was the First Test, due to take place at Ellis Park. Gordon Waddell was out-half with that most durable of scrum-halves, Dickie Jeeps, as his partner. Alun Pask, Mike Campbell-Lamerton and Budge Rogers formed the back row, Keith Rowlands and Bill Mulcahy were in the second row and Syd Millar, Bryn Meredith and Kingsley Jones of Wales were in the front. It was a good pack and I thought it would stand up to the Springboks. It did too in a match that ended in a 3-3 draw.

That game was, in fact, the first international I ever watched, but I was too anxious to enjoy it fully. The Springboks had the better of the first half and their pack, which included Johan Claassen, Frik Du Preez, Doug Hopwood, Mof Myburg, in front of a back line of great strength. John Gainsford got the only score in the first half, a try. We equalised near the end. That game produced a very small number of penalties and was played in a spirit altogether in contrast to the game against Northern Transvaal, though our left winger Niall Brophy got a rough passage and was laid out on at least three occasions.

All things considered, a draw was a satisfactory result for us and we had a most enjoyable match against Natal a few days later, which we won by 13-3. This was the second match I played on tour, so I was still struggling for fitness, but down on the coast I found things much easier than up at Windhoek.

Games at Port Elizabeth and Bloemfontein gave us a win and a draw before we met the Junior Springboks at Pretoria and again this was a game that could be described as rough at times bordering on the crude. The next match against the Combined Services at Potchefstroon, was described by one reporter as 'jungle warfare', a totally apt phrase to describe an encounter in which some of the incidents were disgraceful. We won the match by 20 points to 6 and John Willcox, who wore contact lenses in that match for the first time, kicked three penalty goals for us. There followed two most enjoyable matches against Western Province at Cape Town and South West Districts at Outshoorn and then came the Second Test at Durban.

I had played only four matches on the tour which was now gone well beyond the halfway stage. It was not a very significant contribution, so I was a member of the 'Wednesday' team, and not a very regular member of the side at that. Yet I was beginning to enjoy my rugby and feel fit and I was not having any trouble with the leg.

The Lions made two changes for the Second Test. Dewi Bebb came on at left wing; Brophy was the latest on the injured list and Budge Rogers was also under treatment. He was replaced by Haydn Morgan on the flank. The Springboks also made changes and brought Englebrecht in on one wing and this game saw the debut of that splendid scrum-half Dawi De Villiers.

The game was won by a penalty goal kicked in the second half by out-half Keith Oxlee, a player for whom I acquired profound admiration on that tour and for whom I never lost respect. He was an outstanding player whose talents extended over all aspects of out-half play.

The Lions were very unfortunate to finish on the losing end of that game and the match ended in controversy with the Lions appearing to have scored a push-over try in the last minute. But it was not allowed. Many years later another Test was to end in controversy of even deeper significance, but by then the wheels of fortune were to be moving in a very different direction to the trend the Test series took in 1962.

The win in the Durban Test was vitally important for it gave the Springboks a 1-0 lead and thus considerable advantage in the remaining internationals, of which there were two.

Sharp returned for the next game against Northern Universities, but we had a close call with David Hewitt saving us with a late try that earned a draw. The game that followed is often looked on as the Fifth Test, the match against Transvaal at Ellis Park. To my surprise I was selected and it was to prove a turning point for me. Transvaal were exceptionally strong, but the Lions gave the best display of the tour that afternoon and thrashed Transvaal by 24 points to 3. I will never forget the display given by Bill Mulcahy in that match, he was magnificent and his words of encouragement to me were a great help. Tom Kiernan also played in that game at full-back and Sharp, who had understandably been rather hesitant in the game against Northern Universities, came right back to his very best against Transvaal and scored the majority of our points. Not surprisingly that game had a great influence on the selection for the Third Test at Cape Town and I was delighted to find myself chosen to partner Mulcahy in the second row. Kiernan was at full-back for Willcox and Sharp took over at out-half from Gordon Waddell, who had done such a good job in Sharp's absence.

That Test was both a good experience and an occasion of great sadness for me. We more than held our own and at half-time the score was 3-3. With the game in its closing stages, I felt we might still win it and so square the series. Then a bad mistake left Oxlee in for a crucial try. We tried to run the ball out of a defensive position and Sharp's pass outside did not go to hand, Oxlee gathered the ball and had no difficulty in scoring a try to which he also added the goal points. He in fact scored all South Africa's points in that Test which clinched the series for the Springboks. How much they owed to Oxlee, not alone in terms of his scoring ability, but his tactical kicking and general play in the vital out-half position!

Injuries and the mental and physical strains as the tour neared its end, took the edge off the Lions and we were well and truly hammered in the final Test at Bloemfontein. I played in that game too with Bill Mulcahy on the flank, a circumstance brought about by our injury problems, notably a serious one to Alun Pask in the Third Test when he ended up amongst the spectators.

So it was all over now and on our way home we played and won a match against East Africa in Nairobi.

I don't believe we deserved to lose the Test series 3-0, but I knew in my heart that despite the incredible problems we had faced with injuries, the South Africans were better than us. I got off the plane at London a much wiser young man and definitely a much fitter one than I had been when undertaking the journey out to Rhodesia almost four months earlier.

There were aspects of the tour that were satisfactory; the spirit and management for instance had been good from the word go. The features that had impressed me about the South Africans was their ability to do the basic things so well, to cut out mistakes at the vital moments and to punish our errors. Their application too was impressive. This was my first experience of how wide the difference between law interpretation was in South Africa compared to what I had been used to in Britain and Ireland. Quite apart from interpretation, I found some of the decisions decidedly odd.

If the basic premise of the Springboks play was built on the strength of their forwards, I thought that until the final and humiliating test, our forwards had done extremely well against them. But they had kicked their penalty goals at the vital moments. We had played 24 matches in South Africa, won 15 drew 4 and lost 5; unfortunately three of the losses were in Tests. We had also been forced to call for three replacements on the tour and that was a record at the time for a touring team. But despite all the factors, I also realised that the Springboks were better organised than we were and better able to use their strengths. That, in a word, seemed to reflect coaching methods. Such a word as 'coach' was scarcely used in the corridors of power in our part of the rugby world.

5
What about Meads?

W I T H the Lions tour behind me, I approached the 1962-63 season with more confidence than I had ever known. The postponement of the match against Wales the previous season meant that there would be an international exceptionally early and the match was fixed for Lansdowne Road on 18 November 1962. I was pleased to be selected for the game, my fourth cap for Ireland. There were three new caps in the side; Mick O'Callaghan of the Sunday's Well club in Cork, Dave Kiely of Lansdowne was in the back row and P. J. O'Dwyer of U.C.D. was in the front row with O'Callaghan, which meant that Ronnie Dawson had two new caps on either side of him.

The match was in many respects an academic exercise, for the 1961-62 championship had long since been decided with France the winners. We had been assured of a more doubtful distinction, the wooden spoon, but we felt it would be nice to salvage something having lost the three games we played the previous season. In the long term, a good performance would do much to boost morale for what was to come later that season in the championship.

We did not win, but we did achieve a draw and that was more than a relief to me at least. It was my sixth international, fourth for Ireland, two with the Lions, and I still awaited the alleged feeling of intoxication by finishing on a winning side at international level. The intoxication extracted from a glass, win or lose, was a more common sensation; but having said that, I must add hastily that the popular conception of rugby players training on beer is a long way from the truth.

Certainly many like to relax with a drink after a match and there is always a celebration or commiseration after an international. Yet a great number of players, especially those in the top sphere, do not drink at all. The majority of internationals are moderate drinkers, they would not stay long in their national teams were it otherwise.

The new year of 1963 brought no immediate joy for Ireland as it was the same old story against France in Dublin, when we were comprehensively beaten by 24 points to 5. I say comprehensively, but in fact that was the highest score ever recorded by France against Ireland up to that time; not only that, the margin of 19 points were also the widest against us since we started playing France over fifty years earlier.

It could hardly be said then, that my advent to the Irish side coincided with much prosperity. In fact it was suggested to me that perhaps I was a bit of a jinx. Not being a superstitious individual, I rejected that proposal, but I did begin to wonder if I would ever play on a winning Irish side. There had been a multitude of changes since I had come into the team the previous year; somewhere, someone would soon start wondering about my usefulness.

One of the more disturbing aspects of that heavy defeat against France was the fact that France had been well beaten by Scotland and at Colombes too. We had made five changes from the side that drew with Wales in November and two of the alterations brought in new caps, Pat Casey of Lansdowne on the left wing and John Murray of U.C.D. at out-half. There was a lot of publicity surrounding the selection of Murray as the son of one of Ireland's most famous players, Paul Murray, who played for Ireland in three different positions in the 1930's and also had played for the Lions.

There were a few more alterations for the match against England in Dublin and one of them saw Brian Marshall come in at full-back for Tom Kiernan. Casey was moved into the centre to partner Jerry Walsh, the best mid-field tackler I had seen up to that time, and I have not seen better since. The match ended in a draw, which was something of an achievement for us. It was not a very worthy spectacle if one judges by the reports that followed, one journalist writing that 'both sides were extremely lucky to get nil'. There could not have been more severe criticism than that.

We managed to get nil again against Scotland at Murrayfield when Tom Kiernan returned in place of Marshall at fullback and Tony O'Reilly, dropped against France, came back in the side on the wing in place of Niall Brophy who was injured. It was O'Reilly's 27th cap, not bad for a man whose business commitments even at that time were taking up a considerable amount of his energies. A man of wit no less than wisdom, his rounded talents were later to blossom and take him to the top of a major international company. He also acquired a newspaper, obviously on the basis that if he could not beat them, own them, although that acquisition came when his rugby career was over. More seriously though, O'Reilly is one of those gifted individuals who would succeed no matter what his chosen profession, and even now it is hard to define exactly what his chosen profession may be. At any rate, he was still earning international rugby favours when we met Wales in Cardiff in March 1963 and shared in a great victory for Ireland for we won that day by 14 points to 6. Tom Kiernan played a major part in that win; he converted a try by Pat Casey to give us the lead after Wales had opened the scoring with a try. He then kicked two penalty goals and Mick English dropped a goal. Mick, another with a glib tongue and a faithful son of that great rugby city, Limerick, was a fine footballer and O'Reilly's match when it came to repartee. We might have been short on talent at that time, but not on wit. That afternoon in Cardiff, on a wet and treacherous surface, the Irish forwards gave the Welsh a roasting and the backs did the rest.

So, at long last I savoured that intoxicated feeling that follows an international win, and I seem to recall the soreheaded symptoms of the other sort of intoxication the following morning! The win over Wales lifted us off the bottom of the table and that season Wales took the spoon, while

42

England won the championship; our draw with them in Dublin deprived them of the Triple Crown and the Grand Slam for they ended the season with 7 points out of 8. Incredibly, they have not won the title since.

The question that I have undoubtedly been asked most frequently throughout my international career and indeed since I have retired from the international arena is: 'What about Colin Meads?' I don't suppose there has ever been a more controversial character in international rugby than the New Zealand second row forward. I would doubt too whether there has ever been a better forward in the game's history. Our careers were to run on a parallel course for quite some time, although he was a well established international when I came on the scene in 1962. He went on to play in fifty-five internationals for New Zealand and so became the world's most capped player. I was later to take that record from him, a circumstance that in no way diminished his fame either inside or outside New Zealand. Meads, from that fertile territory in New Zealand, Kings Country, made his international debut in 1957, toured South Africa with the All Blacks in 1960 and so came to Britain and Ireland with Wilson Whineray's Fifth All Blacks in the autumn of 1963 as the holder of twenty-one caps and a growing reputation.

My first encounter with him came at Lansdowne Road on 7 December 1963 in the first international of that tour. The memory of that game will remain with me all my days and my clash with Colin forged a friendship that has ripened through the years. The match against Ireland was the fourteenth of the All Blacks tour and they had won the lot. Not unexpectedly they were the warmest of favourites to beat us and the prophets in general indicated that it was likely to be a victory of handsome proportions. As events transpired, they were right in going for New Zealand. They were wrong, however, in thinking that it would be easy. I have not played in any team at any level that gave more to a game than the Irish side that lost by a single point to New Zealand that December afternoon in Dublin.

43

We went into the match with two new caps on the wings, John Fortune of Clontarf and the young Lansdowne player, Alan Duggan, who was to have an extended career for Ireland and end up as the most prolific try-scorer ever to play for the men in green. Many underestimated the strength of the Irish pack that afternoon and certainly the New Zealanders had reason to appreciate it. P. J. Dwyer, Ronnie Dawson and Ray McLoughlin formed the front row. Bill Mulcahy and myself were in the second row and Eamonn McGuire, Tony O'Sullivan and Noel Murphy completed the unit. The team captaincy had been taken over by scrum-half Jimmy Kelly, who had Mick English as his partner. Tom Kiernan was at full-back and Pat Casey and Jerry Walsh were in the centre.

New Zealand had one newcomer in the pack, prop Ken Gray from Wellington and that was to be the start of a distinguished international career in which Gray emerged in my view as one of the greatest front row forwards the game has known. There were in fact two Meads playing with New Zealand, Colin and his younger brother Stan, another fine player, but comparatively inexperienced at that time.

We conceded height and weight to New Zealand, but little else in the forward exchanges and they had scarcely got under way when I felt the full extent of Colin Meads' experience and his psychology. In the first line-out of the game, I found myself fired three or four yards out of the line. I did not have to exercise my mind to any great degree to know how that came about. I immediately said to myself: 'Now I either live or die today'. I intended to go on living. I must stand up. I realised at once that my survival depended on my reaction, and how I did react is not to be recommended to any young player. The next lineout, I hit Meads as hard as I could and he went down. I clearly remember Wilson Whineray going over and speaking to him. He did not stay down very long; almost immediately there was a ruck, and I got a punch in the jaw. I did not see it delivered, but I had no doubt of its origin. I freely admit I was dazed, yet from that moment to

44

this day, I never again had any physical trouble with Colin Meads.

There are some who will throw up their hands in horror at the thought of one player striking another. I am afraid it does happen in a physical game and forward play in rugby is physical. The laws are such that in congested areas such as ruck and maul, scrum and line-out, there is opportunity for the mischief-maker. Often it is impossible for the referee to see him perpetrate his wrong doings. It is an inescapable fact that at times one has to meet force with force, for if international rugby breeds one thing above all others, it is respect, and an integral part of that respect centres on the ability of a man to match his opponent physically. Much has been made of a frequently used quotation about getting in your retaliation first. I certainly would not set out to provoke a player, nor advocate it, nor seek to win by physical intimidation. On the other hand, it would be untrue to say that it does not happen in rugby and I feel certain in other contact games as well. Yet rugby, for all its physical contact, probably has a better record than any other major game in terms of discipline.

Nonetheless, if a player becomes known as a 'soft touch' there are many who are ready to take advantage of it. That is part of the psychological warfare of all sports. It is not commendable, but it is true. So in a word you have to learn to take care of yourself, and this is especially true against touring teams such as the Springboks and All Blacks, whose game is based so much on the strength and vigour of their forwards.

Colin Meads was as hard a man as I ever encountered. There are some who will tell you he was a dirty player. I cannot subscribe to that view. He was the best, most aggressive, and perhaps the most totally committed player that I have opposed, and I think it is within the terms of the last mentioned attribute that he got a reputation that is ill deserved. At times Meads did silly things that he did not have to do. Perhaps reflex action on occasion accounted for indiscretions. That may be taken as a flaw in his make-up, yet his indiscretions

45

were within the context of a dedication that was over-zealous. He knew his rugby and his opponents as no man I have ever encountered knew them. He was a man of few words but deep reflection; if he knew he had the better of an opponent he was ruthless in putting him down.

I did not learn all I knew about Meads on my first engagement with him in 1963, but during many other matches both in New Zealand and in Britain and Ireland. I finished on the losing side against Meads more times than on the victorious, but I still believe that my first match against him should have been won by Ireland.

Nevertheless all the things I had been told about New Zealand prior to that first international came true. We would have beaten any other side in the world that day but New Zealand. Their support play, so much a feature of their game, was magnificent. Their ability to drive forward in the rucks and mauls and to cut off danger by intelligent anticipation were all in evidence. But they did not get enough of the ball to weave their patterns of destruction.

We led 5-3 at half-time, John Fortune having scored a try and Tom Kiernan converted it. Kel Tremain scored a try for New Zealand, after Stan Meads had done the bulk of the work. Mick English was only inches wide with a dropped goal attempt, but we thoroughly deserved to be in the lead at the interval. We had played with the wind in the first half and the feeling in the team was that we could win, but there must be no let up in concentration or no slackening in our defence. The back row that afternoon was superb and for over twenty minutes in the second period we held on to our lead. Then Don Clarke kicked a penalty goal for New Zealand. Even so we were still there with more than an outside chance and just before the end drove forward over the New Zealand line, but the 'try' was disallowed by the English referee, Mr Keenan.

It goes into the record books as another 'glorious' Irish failure. I suppose we have had more 'glorious' failures than any other country, but that afternoon, we did take the glory even if New Zealand took the spoils. I think that too often we sought to take glory after defeat and good performances, when search and analysis would have given us the answers to narrow defeats. Mistakes at crucial moments and an inability at times to press home advantages probably accounted for many losses written off as moral victories. But that lesson was to be brought home to us at a later date, primarily by more careful study of method and proper coaching.

That New Zealand side lost only one game on tour, to Newport. I played against them again for Ulster; this time Colin Meads was not playing and they won easily. Once more they made a profound impression on me, even more than the Springboks had done during the Lions tour in the summer of 1962.

I had now played against all the major rugby playing nations and I formed the opinion that the New Zealanders were the most complete in method. Subsequent events did not alter that view. They are the hardest to beat; their forwards are generally just as strong physically as the Springboks, but in my experience they are better technically. Behind the scrum, their game may be described as more mechanical than flamboyant, but it is generally both impressive and extremely effective. They have never won a Test series in South Africa and that underlines the magnitude of the achievement of those who have. I think climatic conditions no less than the durability, character and talents of the Springboks are a factor in this. I would like to see South Africa and New Zealand play a Test series in Britain. If I had to stake a lot on the outcome, I would have to put my money on the New Zealanders.

After such a good display against the All Blacks, there was an air of confidence that Ireland would do well in the championship and such was the start to the campaign for us that immediately there was talk of the Triple Crown and the Championship. We went to Twickenham with a team that contained only one new cap, Mike Gibson, the young man who a few weeks previously had set Twickenham alight with a magnificent performance for Cambridge University against Oxford in the 'Varsity match.

There can scarcely have been a better international debut than Gibson's. He tore England apart with brilliant running, handling and passing. We led by only 3-0 at half-time, but the trend before the interval looked distinctly promising for us. Bill Mulcahy had again taken over the captaincy from Jimmy Kelly and he was quite right when he told us at the interval that if we could get possession, the backs would do the rest. They did, thanks mainly to Gibson.

Gibson was opposed that day by Tom Brophy, who was also making his debut for England. He had the reputation of being a very elusive runner and so he was. But it was Gibson whose name was on the lips of the spectators when it was all over and we had won by 18 points to 5.

Gibson had created the first try for us scored by Noel Murphy. England hit back in the second half and led briefly, but then Kevin Flynn got a try for us and Tom Kiernan converted. After that, there was only one team in it and Pat Casey got a try that will be remembered as long as the game is played. Kiernan converted that too and then Jimmy Kelly engineered another try for Flynn. It was a great performance, all the more so as John Fortune had been injured and was off the field for a period in the second half, while Gibson had severe cramp in the closing stages of the game.

Now there was definite hope that at long last we would take the championship. We had Scotland and Wales in Dublin, so the signs were right. The match against Scotland as it transpired was a disaster. We had two changes; Ken Houston came in on the wing for Fortune and P. J. Dwyer replaced Mick O'Callaghan at prop.

Nothing went right for us from the start of that game. We were beaten forward by the Scots and not helped by the fact that Ray McLoughlin limped through most of the game. Scotland were 6 up at half-time with two penalty goals and the only reply we could manage was a penalty from Kiernan, who that afternoon was like the rest of us, out of touch, with his kicking attempts. We rallied near the end, but an injury to Gerry Culliton was a severe blow. We had been out-played by the Scots and could not offer excuse or complaint about the justice of the result.

6
Dropped by Ireland

So in the space of a fortnight, Ireland had taken the rapid step from the sublime to the downright poor and when the team to meet Wales in Dublin was announced, there were four changes; not surprisingly, three of the alterations were made in the pack and one of those to go was McBride. I cannot say that I was surprised for I had had a poor game against Scotland and indeed for some strange reason I had in fact begun to lose form after the match against New Zealand.

My place went to the University College Cork player, Mick Leahy, a member of the Garda (the Irish Police) and apparently an accomplished boxer who was a good and abrasive second row forward. Tom Kiernan went too and was replaced by Fergus Keogh, a full-back with a tremendous reputation as a place-kicker. Ronnie Dawson and Ray McLoughlin were also discarded and replaced by Paddy Lane, like myself a farmer and now the president of the Irish Farmers Association, and Al Moroney.

As events transpired I could not have played even if I had been selected for I had a leg injury, but that had nothing whatsoever to do with my omission. I was dropped after nearly three seasons in the national team, and it hurt. I was not to know such humiliation again during my international career, but the injury I had at the time, just below the knee, has troubled me periodically ever since and I have from that date, worn a protective bandage.

Ireland lost the match against Wales and so the selectors rang the changes again for the visit to Paris. I was recalled. We had reason to have doubts about our engagement at

Colombes Stadium, for Paris had not proved very gay for the Irish as we had not won there for thirteen years. We were not favoured to break that sequence either for our Springtime engagement. The match was in the middle of April and we did not disappoint the prophets.

I have always felt that France are more difficult to beat late in the season, for the hard and dry ground that one inevitably gets at that time of year is very suited to the type of game France like to play. We had Ronnie Dawson, Mick O'Callaghan and Alan Duggan back in the team. It was in fact Dawson's last game for Ireland and I am afraid not a very happy experience. The French gave us a terrible thrashing by 27 points to 6, the biggest win they had ever recorded against Ireland. Surprisingly they dropped André Boniface for the game and perhaps it was well for Ireland that he did not play. Those who did performed a very good demolition job on us without the assistance of Boniface, a splendid player and one of two brothers to play for France. Guy, unfortunately, died tragically at a very early age.

So in two years, France beat us by record scores, having run up 24 points in Dublin the previous year, now they had done even better. Things had come a long way since their hesitant start in the international arena at the beginning of the century. And the great promise that the season held out after our display against the All Blacks and our tremendous win at Twickenham, had turned sour and we eventually ended up at the bottom of the championship table.

When the 1964-65 season started, events of great significance took place. We were not aware of all of them at the time, but the nomination of Ray McLoughlin as captain of the team to meet France in Dublin, our first match that season, suggested a new era was about to dawn. McLoughlin had very specific ideas about what was required in the way of preparation and he quickly put them into practice. I deal with the McLoughlin era in more detail later on, but he made a reasonable beginning for we drew with France 3-3 in Dublin and that amounted to a good start considering we had lost to them by so heavy a margin in the final game of our programme in 1964.

In addition to the new captain, Ireland brought in five new caps for the match against France and so started the careers of some of the greatest players to wear the green jersey. Four of them were to earn recognition for the Lions, one Ken Kennedy went on to win a world record of 45 caps for a hooker. He was a young medical student at Queen's University when he won his first cap and another youngster from Queen's, scrum-half Roger Young, also made his debut in that game. He was to become Ireland's most capped player at scrum-half. Ronnie Lamont, and Mick Doyle came into the back row for their first caps and Sean McHale, a fine prop forward from Lansdowne, was in the front row. Kennedy, Lamont, Doyle and Young, all won Lions tours and while McHale was not so honoured nor did he have a lengthy international career, he played a dozen games for Ireland and helped fashion the new era.

Our next assignment under McLoughlin was against England in Dublin, a game crucial for both as we had dropped a point against France and England had lost decisively to Wales. The loser here could bid farewell to the championship and McLoughlin did not figure on being the loser.

My abiding memory of that game is of a high wind. It was basically a forward battle which we had dictated but without profit until about a quarter of an hour from the end. Ronnie Lamont got a try and Tom Kiernan kicked the conversion. The try came from a break by Roger Young and Kiernan's conversion was, if my memory is correct, from near the touchline. He missed a very easy penalty subsequently, but his performance on a day calculated to test any full-back, was well nigh immaculate. I wonder if there has ever been a more sure fielder of the high ball? We had a new cap in that match, Paddy McGrath from University College Cork on the wing.

Ronnie Lamont was missing for the game against Scotland and we had Henry Wall at number eight, while Jerry Walsh was back in the three-quarter line. This was my fourth appearance against Scotland and thus far I had finished on the losing side on every occasion. Not so that afternoon at Murrayfield, for we beat the Scots in every phase of play especially up front, and Ireland scored a great 16-6 win.

So now everything was set for the Triple Crown battle in Cardiff between Ireland and Wales. Things had come a long way in a short time and Ireland had made the transition smoothly enough from the bottom to top of the table, though as yet we had won neither crown nor championship. Cardiff on 13 March would decide such issues, though Wales' game against France that season was not until the end of March. If we beat Wales, however, that game would be of no more than academic interest as far as the championship was concerned. I shall never forget the build-up. Just about everyone in Ireland seemed to be heading for Cardiff and I think a fair proportion of them thought I was going to supply them with tickets. McLoughlin's pre-match analysis was if anything almost too detailed. He honestly believed we would win and so did most of the team. I am not sure if all members of the side went all the way with McLoughlin in his method of preparation, but time might prove him right, while if we were to lose, which eventually we did, it was not necessarily a reason for suggesting he was wrong, though he knew and I knew that was how it would be interpreted by some in the corridors of power.

David Hewitt was recalled for the game which was played in almost continuous rain before as passionate a crowd as one could possibly imagine. One always gets the impression at the Arms Park that the Welsh do not so much hope to win as look upon it as a divine right, and their record there in recent times has almost given substance to that belief.

From the outset things went wrong for us. Kiernan missed a penalty from almost in front of the posts and one could scarcely say he was granted the customary silence afforded to kickers in those days. He took the kick to an incessant chorus of booing. Other than in France, I had not experienced anything like this in my career up to that time. The practice of booing opposing kickers is regrettably now all too prevalent.

It was not only the spectators however who stepped over the brink that afternoon; some of the Welsh players got caught up with the highly emotional nature of the occasion and acted in a manner calculated to lead to a breach of the peace. We might be beaten, but we were not going to be intimidated. I would point out that not all the indiscretions were on the Welsh side and indeed before half-time the referee called both captains and told them to instruct their teams to cool down and play rugby. His lecture and admonishment had the necessary effect.

It looked like a blank scoreline at half-time and then that splendid little out-half, David Watkins, later to turn to rugby league with great success, scored a try for Wales, and Terry Price, also to take the road 'North' to the rugby league scene, converted. A try by Dewi Bebb gave Wales a 8-0 lead and it was hard to visualise the Welsh losing such an advantage. A penalty by Kiernan gave us some hope, but alas not for long, as Price, a wonderful kicker of the ball, dropped a magnificent goal for Wales.

If we were at the bottom of the mountain, we were not ready to surrender. Kevin Flynn scored a try and Kiernan again converted so it was now 11-8 and there were still five minutes to go. I remember very well Ray McLoughlin's urgings and promptings. He told us we could still do it, but this time he was wrong and there was more than a little relief on the terraces when, after Wales had withstood a period of intense Irish pressure, Price kicked a penalty to tie it up for Wales, who were champions and Triple Crown winners whatever was to happen in Paris. Scrum-half Clive Rowlands had led them to the twin triumph and his tactical kicking, not perhaps the type of game on which Wales have built their reputation for the flamboyant, had played a major part in steering them to success on this occasion. So Ireland had finished the season with five points, and that was tantamount to a dramatic improvement on recent years whatever about the disappointments of Cardiff.

It would be untrue to say that there was not criticism of McLoughlin's leadership in the immediate aftermath of that game. He was accused of being too intense and of trying to reduce the game to a formula, sacrificing freedom for theory. In my book, he had done a wonderful job in a short time even if he had made mistakes. The overall good by far outweighed any errors he had made on or off the field.

Ireland still had another game to play that season, for the Springboks were due on a short tour of Ireland and Scotland, a reciprocal tour for games played in South Africa. It proved a traumatic experience for the Springboks who opened their tour with a draw against Combined Provinces in Belfast. I had the pleasure to play for the Provinces and felt after the game that Ireland had a really wonderful chance of beating South Africa for the first time the following week in Dublin. I was strengthened in that belief when the Combined Irish Universities side beat the South Africans in Limerick four days before the international. How appropriate it was that the first win by an Irish team over a touring side should have been recorded on Munster soil, where so many great efforts had been put in by successive Munster teams against Wallabies, All Blacks and Springboks with no greater reward than the near miss and the hard luck tale.

Ireland met South Africa on 4 April 1965 at Lansdowne Road. There were some old friends and old foes in the Springboks pack, such as Kuhn and Malan. Hannes Marais was also in the front row and I was to get to know him much better at a later date when he and I would be opposing captains in a Test series. Behind the scrum, Englebrecht, John Gainsford and Dawie De Villiers were there to lend their talents to the challenge. It was likely to be hard—is it ever anything else against the Springboks in an international?

How I wanted to win this match! I had been on the receiving end three years previously with the Lions and finished on the losing side in the two Tests I played. A short tour is a far cry from a full one when team work can be established and a pattern of play emerges. On the quick short visit, there is little time to work on problems and all touring teams have them in some shape, at times in a wide variety.

It is true that the South Africans came at a time when their own season at home was only just about to begin, but there had been similar circumstances in the past and they did more than survive on British and Irish soil. That afternoon they did not survive for we won and the journalist who wrote: 'Spring, summer, autumn or winter, the pack that can stand up to the Springboks deserve nothing but the highest praise and Ireland did more than stand up to them on this occasion', made fair comment. We played into a strong wind in the first half and were level 3-3 at the interval; we had scored a try through Paddy McGrath and they had a penalty goal from David Stewart. We had, it is true, a few close calls near our line, but we held them off.

Now with the wind at our backs and our confidence mounting, we did most of the attacking, but ironically it was the Springboks who scored, a try from one of their wings. Kiernan, however, brought us level with a penalty goal and then Mike Gibson scored what we all thought was a try, but which the referee did not and Gibson was whistled back for some infringment by himself or some other of us. But it was Kiernan who had the last word with a penalty that is still talked about in detail by all who saw it. The ball seemed to take an eternity of time to reach its objective, but it slipped between the posts and there followed a deafening roar. We had done it at last.

That win against the Springboks should be put in its right perspective and few outside Ireland have done so. The magnitude of the achievement in beating South Africa can be assessed against the fact that only once had the Springboks been beaten in an international by one of the home countries, Scotland in 1906. Wales have not to this day beaten the Springboks and England managed it for the first time in 1970. It had been accomplished by a combination of the youthful and the experienced. Lamont, Gibson, Kennedy, Doyle,

McGrath, McHale of the younger school had joined forces with Kiernan, Flynn, Noel Murphy, Ray McLoughlin and Mulcahy, to mention a few of the more experienced campaigners. For me there was one personal note of sadness attached to the game, for it was Bill Mulcahy's last appearance for Ireland. Could there have been a higher note on which to go out? Yes, a Triple Crown win a few weeks previously; but it is not every day a man can say he finished his career by playing on a side that beat South Africa. It was my privilege to have played with Mulcahy, my extreme good fortune to have partnered him in the second row of the Irish scrum.

Yet the departure of Bill was to bring in another great player and forge for me a great friendship with another farmer's son, this time from the unlikely rugby territory of Connemara, the native heath of the young medical student from University College Galway who was my partner in Paris in January 1966, Mick Molloy. It was the beginning of a great career and the first offering from the Galwayman of what in my opinion has been a signal contribution to Irish rugby. Molloy, no more than myself did not make a winning debut that day in Paris. We went down by 11-6. Not then an auspicious start to the championship for us.

A draw with England in Dublin also meant the end of Triple Crown ambitions. The two results combined to put pressures on McLoughlin's captaincy and give ammunition to those of the officials who would gladly see him lose the leadership. What I consider to have been the final blow for Ray came when we lost to Scotland in Dublin by 11 points to 3. I had another new partner that afternoon, Ollie Waldron, a young student from Cork, then playing with Oxford University. He was later to leave a greater imprint on the game in the prop forward berth. Aidan Brady was in as hooker for Ken Kennedy, while Barry Bresnihan, who had made his debut against England, was in the centre at the start of another career that amounted to a great contribution to Ireland and the Lions.

57

I was not surprised when McLoughlin lost the captaincy for the game against Wales. It was taken over by Tom Kiernan and he led us to a 9-6 win. A welcome victory it was too, our only success of the season, in a year when the Lions were due to go to New Zealand during the summer.

7
All Black and Blue

J u s t prior to the selection of the party to tour Australia and
New Zealand in the summer of 1966, there had been much
speculation in the press and indeed among the players as to
who would captain the side. Ray McLoughlin had been suggested by many at the start of the season as the likely captain;
but happenings in Ireland, his subsequent replacement as
Ireland's captain for the game against Wales, obviously ruined
his chances. Alun Pask of Wales was another strong candi-
date, and I thought Pask would get the job when McLoughlin
was virtually ruled out by the action of the Irish selectors.

When the appointment was eventually announced it was
greeted with astonishment in most quarters. The man chosen
was Mike Campbell-Lamerton of London-Scottish and Scotland. What was really incredible about Mike's appointment
was the fact that he had not even led his own national side
that season.

The management structure consisted of Des O'Brien, a
member of Ireland's great Triple Crown winning teams of
1948-49, as manager, and John Robins, the former Welsh
international, was assistant manager. He also had a loose brief
as coach, for as yet the concept of coaching had not been
accepted by the Four Home Unions, and suggestions that John
would be coach were whispered rather than spoken. The squad
contained some truly great players, but in fact only one
member who had previously toured New Zealand with the
Lions, Ireland's flanker, Noel Murphy.

I was delighted to be chosen and looked forward to the tour
eagerly. I had plenty of my compatriots with me too. In

addition to Murphy, Ken Kennedy, Ray McLoughlin, Ronnie Lamont, Jerry Walsh, Roger Young and Mike Gibson were all in the party while there were several players from the other countries whom I knew well and respected. Dewi Bebb of Wales, Stewart Watkins, Mike Weston and David Watkins were just a few of the backs, while in the pack we had the makings of a really formidable unit and an immense amount of international experience.

However, it would be less than honest were I not to admit that this tour was doubtlessly the most unhappy period of my rugby life. Without offering individual criticism, it seemed to me from the outset that the management was quite unable to cope with the demands of so arduous a tour. I also had the impression of differences of opinion with the management and the more the tour progressed, the firmer that impression became.

Things started well enough from a playing viewpoint for we did well in Australia, winning seven of our eight matches and drawing one. In addition we won both Tests, a circumstance that owed nothing to me for I did not play in either of them. Campbell-Lamerton and Brian Price of Wales were the second row in the first and the same combination was retained for the second Test. I had no complaints on that score for Campbell-Lamerton was the captain and Brian Price was certainly among the best line-out jumpers in the world. Throughout the Australian part of the tour I did not in fact play in my normal position more than once. I was picked both at number eight and on the flank. I did not particularly mind for what was considered correct for the team was acceptable to me.

Jerry Walsh had to return home shortly after the tour started because of the death of his father. Another Irishman, Barry Bresnihan, a good and strong centre, was called out as replacement, while Mike Gibson did not play in Australia due to examination commitments.

Any complacency engendered by the success of the team in Australia was rapidly removed after the first match in New

Zealand. We knew this would be a different ball game and we had that lesson hammered home when Southland beat us at Invercargill by 14 points to 8. In retrospect, I think that this defeat brought with it an erosion of confidence that was never checked and in fact became more pronounced as the tour progressed. We lost the third game of the tour as well to Otago, and then Wellington gave us a good hammering. We won a few games and then drew with the Bay of Plenty before getting home narrowly against North Auckland. The next game was the first Test at Dunedin and events immediately before that took a turn that taught me a lesson. The spirit in the side was not high; there were obvious disagreements within the management and to cap all the problems, John Robins damaged an Achilles tendon and had to go to hospital.

One thing that stands out in my mind was a remark from a New Zealander shortly after we arrived in the country. 'You had a great record in Australia and I saw you play there', he said, 'but you will see what rugby is about from now on'. He was right. When the pressure came on us, we did not have the qualities required to meet it.

There was a lack of commitment from some players and I attribute that primarily to a breakdown in management. Players broke up into groups with national boundaries often the demarcation line. Many players felt that they had not been given a fair chance to stake a claim for a Test place and it was hard to argue against some of them. Mike Campbell-Lamerton was asked to bear a tremendous burden, far too great for any one man to carry.

There is often talk on tour about Wednesday teams and Saturday teams, with the Saturday men the recognised stars. Never had this been more obvious, and the final straw came when shortly before the first Test, it was decided that a Test panel would be taken away for special preparation with the rest of the players left to fend for themselves. My selection for the panel did not diminish my disagreement with such an action. A touring squad is a team or nothing. We even had the ludicrous rule of a ten o'clock curfew being put on players.

To treat grown men in this way and expect commitment from them shows just how sad the whole scene had become.

Not surprisingly, we were devastated in the first Test, New Zealand winning by 20 points to 3. But for the displays of Dewi Bebb and Mike Gibson in the backs and Ronnie Lamont and a few other forwards who were outstanding in the pack, the score would probably have reached record proportions. Roger Young the scrum-half was playing in his first Test match and he got a real gruelling yet he stood up to everything thrown at him.

After the humiliation by a New Zealand team that showed the true greatness of All Black forward play, a few of the players got together with Mike Campbell-Lamerton. Noel Murphy, who knew more than any of us about New Zealand rugby, spoke frankly, as did Ray McLoughlin and a few others. Campbell-Lamerton took the courageous decision to drop himself from the second Test side, and Delme Thomas and myself formed the second row. We did reasonably well in that game and in fact led for quite a while before the All Blacks pulled away to win by four points. At least there had been marked improvement from the humiliation of Dunedin, but things had gone too far to hope for a recovery against a country that had so many great forwards and backs who did not make mistakes, even if they did not exactly set the world alight with their spirit of adventure.

Despite all our troubles on that tour, there were some of our backs who showed the All Blacks what flair behind the scrum was all about. Gibson was brilliant and Colin McFadyean, Stuart Wilson, Dewi Bebb and David Watkins showed a willingness and ability that was markedly absent in the play of the New Zealand backs. The irony of the whole affair was that despite the fact that New Zealand won all four Tests and in fact became the first country to achieve such a feat in a four match Test series anywhere, there was a lot of soul-searching in New Zealand. Many were not satisfied with the play of the New Zealand backs. They were either limited or not prepared to take any chances in attack. Certainly they were at best stereotyped in attack and the backs did not in general respond to the work of their brilliant forwards. And how brilliant some of them were! Colin Meads, his brother Stan, Brian Lochore, Ken Gray, Kel Tremain, Wacka Nathan —there was not one in any of the Test packs the All Blacks fielded who was other than thoroughly well versed in the needs and totally competent in carrying out his brief. Not only were there no weak links, the whole chain was incredibly strong.

We lost the third Test and then the whitewash was completed in the fourth Test in Auckland. That final game took place on 10 September, so by then we had been away from home well over four months. Furthermore we were scheduled to play in Canada on the homeward journey. Like much else on that unfortunate tour, it was far too long and contributed to the catalogue of disaster.

I was certainly convinced that the attitude and approach which Ray McLoughlin had tried to instil into his players for Ireland was more than ever right. He spoke an immense amount of sense on that tour and so also did Noel Murphy. Regrettably, too few were prepared to listen to them. Too many had opted out long before the tour was over and I felt especially sorry for Mike Campbell-Lamerton who, I believe, lost over three stone on the tour, not surprisingly.

The apportionment of blame may be easy in retrospect, but basically I think the whole approach was wrong. The truth was that we were light years behind the All Blacks in method and application. Their game was developing through good organisation and coaching, and those aspects allied to the tremendous physical strength and natural ability of their forwards, was opening up a gap even wider than had obtained in the past.

There were, however, some good things to emanate from this tour. If it did nothing else, it convinced many people at home that something had to be done and it was a matter of the utmost urgency. Men like Ronnie Dawson had come back from New Zealand in 1959 and issued the warnings that

63

we needed a more thorough approach. Dawson and others were cast in the roles of prophets of doom. Now maybe the doubters would realise that doomsday was at hand.

I was not sorry to say goodbye to New Zealand in 1966 despite the hospitality of our hosts which was never less than splendid. The 1966 Lions had been an unlucky team, but they had also been ill-prepared for what they were required to do. Yet the tour had its light-hearted moments, many of them provided by that great Welsh character, Howard Norris, and things can never be dull for very long with players like Ray McLoughlin around, although like several others, he had problems caused by injury.

I had an important date on my return for I was due to be married on 22 October and that did not leave much time for preparations. Indeed, one of the few tasks I had to perform was to get myself a best man and even this job I left almost to the last minute. I realised the urgency one night late in the tour and went to Ronnie Lamont's room and asked him if he would like to accompany me up the aisle. He gladly accepted. He swears that at 3:00 a.m. one morning, I dashed into his room, woke him up and made the request with a ring of urgency and desperation in my voice. It's a good story, but not accurate enough for the record!

On the way home from New Zealand, we stopped off at San Francisco. After coming from a country like New Zealand where rugby is a way of life for almost every man, woman, and child, I was made very conscious that we were now in a new environment. I was holding a large Maori ceremonial staff which I had got in New Zealand and when I walked up the steps of the plane, the hostess, after welcoming me on board asked, 'if I would like to put my rugby stick at the back of the plane'. Need I add she was not a New Zealander! In many ways that incident was more revealing than I at first realised, for it made me aware that the approach in New Zealand is perhaps too intense on the terraces and on the field. Maybe rugby is a coin of too high a value there?

My next assignment after that tour was another moment

The beginning and the end : Above, our school group at Moneyglass. My younger brother, Tom, who was drowned, is on my right, one of our teachers, Mrs Wilson, on left. Below with Eamonn Andrews on *This is Your Life*.

The Irish party that toured Australia in 1967—the first team from the Home Countries ever to win an international match in the Southern Hemisphere. The management team of Jamsey Maher, Eugene Davy and Harry McKibbon are in the centre row.

The Irish team in the Argentine taken during the 1970 tour.

Gareth Edwards gets the ball away from my feet, with Colin Meads
restrained by Sean Lynch, during the 1971 Test series in New Zealand.

Relaxing off the field in South Africa (above)
and New Zealand (below).

COLORSPORT

A word of encouragement to the

Now look here, you blokes . . .

That's not the way . . .

We've got to get tighter.

You get what I mean don't you?

Now I'm sure we've got it!

NORTHERN ADVOCATE, WHANGAREI

IRISH PRESS

Two memorable occasions. Our wedding day, and
with my mother after receiving the MBE.

In jubilant mood after the third Test against South Africa, 1974.

Admiring the collection of rugby souvenirs at Jan Ellis's shop in Winntou during the 1974 Lions tour. Left to right: Ian McGeechan, myself, Andy Ripley, Jan Ellis, Gordon Brown and Gareth Edwards.

that set my nerves tingling—my wedding day. Penny, with her customary efficiency had made all the arrangements, so on 22 October I married the girl that I had won on the toss of a coin the night I first played in a final Irish trial January 1962. I was accompanied that night four years previously by a friend, Jim Kyle. We had a blind date with two girls, one was Penny Michael and the other was Zandra Stevens. We tossed a coin as to who would go with who and I won Penny. No gambler has ever had a luckier break. Zandra was Penny's bridesmaid and I remember wondering that morning how things would have turned out had Jim won Penny in the toss?

I did not have much rest away from the game, for Australia were on tour in Britain and Ireland and I played against them for Ulster early in December of 1966. We drew 6-6, a satisfactory result against a team that had a lot of good players and had in fact beaten Wales at the Arms Park, Cardiff. Subsequently they lost narrowly to Scotland and played brilliantly in beating England at Twickenham before they met Ireland at Lansdowne Road in January. We beat them by 15 points to 8 and the impression I had got in Australia some seven months earlier was confirmed. They had some really good backs but their forward play was rather loose.

A young student from Derry, then at Newcastle University, made his debut for Ireland that day. The player was number eight, Ken Goodall, and if that afternoon he did not set the world alight, he was to develop into one of the great players of my era before he turned professional in 1970.

Ireland had another debutant that afternoon too in the Dolphin prop, Phil O'Callaghan. A strong and durable performer, no one would ever be in any doubt where he came from once he opened his mouth. He has, I think, the most pronounced Cork accent I have ever heard. He also has a ready turn of wit which we were to appreciate in the days ahead.

One notable absentee from the team against Australia was Ray McLoughlin. He was having trouble with a knee injury, and together with his business commitments both were to keep him out of international rugby for five years, though at the time no one realised his absence would be for quite so long. When he did return in 1971, at over 30 years of age, he showed the courage, character and tremendous ability we all knew he possessed.

Noel Murphy was Ireland's new captain and there were hopes that we would mount a championship challenge. There was a lot of experience in the side and the younger players who had come into the team over the past two years were developing into players of great skill.

Our first game was against England and it went the way of so many of our English encounters at that time. We had more than enough of the play to win and ended up as losers, with Colin McFadyean getting a decisive try for England in circumstances that were, to say the least, fortunate.

Yet there were good things to come. We went to Murrayfield and beat Scotland narrowly in a game notable for the debut of Sandy Carmichael for Scotland. Sandy is still around and now the world's most capped prop forward. He must also rank with the best the game has produced.

We went to Cardiff and beat Wales, a rare enough happening to make it notable. We got home by a try, scored by Alan Duggan. So the defeat against England had cost us the Triple Crown. As I said, we had reason to remember McFadyean's try which came in the closing seconds of the game after an Irish passing movement had broken down and McFadyean booted the ball ahead and then won the race to the line.

The last game was against France in Dublin and both countries had a chance to win the championship. France had lost to Scotland but had beaten Wales and England. They beat us decisively with the famous Camberabero brothers Guy and Lilian, at half-back for France, playing major roles in the win. That French team had a magnificent back line with Jean Gachassin, Claude Dourthe, Jean-Pierre Lux, and Christian Darrouy, a threequarter line of sheer brilliance when things were going right. Behind them that afternoon was Pierre Villepreux. That was his international debut and the first of many outstanding games he was to play for his country.

66

So France were champions and they thoroughly deserved to be. Yet we were left to reflect once more on the might-have-beens. But the season was not yet over for Ireland as we were off for the first time to Australia on a six match tour in May.

8

A Notable First

I w a s delighted to be selected for the party, which was due to be led by Noel Murphy. However, he was forced to withdraw from the travelling party for domestic reasons. At one time I had contemplated not going; I was not long married and felt that it might be unfair to Penny to go off on tour just over six months after our marriage and at a time when we were building a home. She would not hear of it, however, an attitude that was typical of her.

We had several uncapped players in our party which was managed by Eugene Davy, a legendary figure in Irish rugby and a magnificent player in the late twenties and early thirties at centre and out-half. He was now a much respected legislator and his assistant was Des McKibbin, a member of a famous Irish rugby family. He was a former international and a brother of Harry who had been assistant manager of the Lions in South Africa in 1962 and now an eminent legislator too. Tom Kiernan took over the leadership of the side.

Kiernan was one of several very experienced backs in the party. It also included Niall Brophy, Barry Bresnihan, Alan Duggan, Mike Gibson, Pat McGrath, Jerry Walsh, and John Murray, who had made one appearance for Ireland a few years previously at out-half. The only notable absentee from the backs was Roger Young, who could not travel. The scrum-halves were Brendan Sherry of Terenure and the young University College Cork player, Liam Hall. Sherry had played two games that season for Ireland.

The pack had a hard core of experience allied to the talents of some very young and promising material. Mick Molloy,

68

now developed into a really formidable second row, Ken Kennedy, Ken Goodall, Sean McHale, Mick Doyle, Phil O'Callaghan were in the party as were prop Sammy Hutton, who had come into the Irish side that season, and Terry Moore, a big and strong number eight from the Highfield club. He was uncapped as were flanker Jim Flynn, a brother of Kevin, and Denis Hickie from St Mary's. The second hooker was Locky Butler, from Blackrock College. He had won a cap in 1960 and then claimed the Irish record for being substitute, at the last count his claim had gone into the forties. Locky was never stuck for a word, whether it was to referee or opponent, it is not unknown for him to talk to his colleagues on and off the field either!

It was a tremendously happy party and the camp followers who made the trip certainly got something to remember. Among them was Dr Jamesy Maher and his presence, as events developed, proved crucial in our historic Test win over Australia. There were three Irish journalists on the tour; Peter McMullen, then rugby correspondent of *The Belfast Telegraph;* Fred Cogley of *Radio Telefís Éireann*; and Paul MacWeeney of *The Irish Times*. It was good to have them along and I think we made their long journey worthwhile.

We started the tour by beating Queensland at Brisbane and then lost to New South Wales in Sydney. At the time, some saw that as an important psychological win for the Australians. However, by the time the Test match came we had recorded another win, against New South Wales Country Districts and we had also picked up a few injury problems. Foremost in this respect was an injury to Brendan Sherry, who had cartilage trouble and Jamesy Maher performed miracles in getting him on the field for the international. Ken Goodall was also not quite right. Then Barry Bresnihan, who had been selected for the game, had to withdraw so Paddy McGrath was switched from wing to centre and Niall Brophy came in on the wing.

The conditions were really tough for players, the vast majority of whom had never experienced anything like them. The game was played on the Sydney Cricket Ground, the temperature was in the eighties and the pitch was as hard as the road. Despite our problems, we were well prepared. Kiernan was proving a great captain and he coached the backs. Des McKibbin and myself looked after the forwards and it was my job to lead the pack. The match was a special occasion for Kiernan as he was equalling the world record of 33 international caps for a full-back. Never was so auspicious an occasion celebrated in more fitting fashion for he was magnificent that afternoon under the Sydney sun.

We took an early lead when Sherry, who was clearly impaired by his knee trouble, made an opening for Jerry Walsh to score a try. Kiernan added the conversion. We led 5-0 at half time and then shortly after the interval, Kiernan dropped a great goal. But we were not home yet for Australia's brilliant scrum-half, Ken Catchpole, scored a try which was converted. Now it was all to play for. Sherry, who as the match progressed was able to do little more than put the ball in the scrum and pass it because of his knee trouble, had to go off. Mick Doyle went to scrum-half and did a great job. But the work on the seven forwards was a load we were finding it difficult to carry. Terry Moore, winning his first cap, did very well at number eight, while Goodall was magnificent in defence. Jamesy Maher eventually got Sherry back into the fray. We had managed to score a try about five minutes after Australia had got their five points so we had something in the bank, after McGrath had stretched our lead from a tenuous 8-5 advantage to a more comfortable 11-5.

With Sherry back, we held on for a great victory. That win was the first ever recorded in the Southern Hemisphere by any of the home countries in an international, an historic occasion in every way. It was so good to be Irish in Sydney that night and for a few nights afterwards. We lost to Sydney three days after the international, but ended the tour with a win over Victoria. It was by any standards a highly successful tour; we had achieved the main purpose, a win in the international, and in addition, I think we had proved worthy ambassadors on and off the field for rugby in the home countries.

The All Blacks were due to visit Britain and Ireland in the autumn of 1967. The tour arose through the cancellation of a series against South Africa who refused to allow Maoris the full facilities afforded other players in the New Zealand party and quite rightly paid the penalty when New Zealand declined to have anything to do with the tour.

Ireland did not in fact meet Brian Lochore's Sixth All Blacks. The games due to take place in Ireland were cancelled because of an outbreak of foot and mouth disease in Britain and the Irish agricultural authorities were afraid that the disease might be brought to Ireland with the consequent disastrous results. As a farmer's son, I cannot say I disagreed with the request which was honoured.

It was, however, a great pity that we did not have the pleasure of meeting that All Blacks side, considered by many to be the best they had ever seen. If there were those who believed the visions of New Zealand rugby were not broad enough during the Lions visit in 1966, Lochore's team went a long way towards removing any disenchantment. They played eleven games, won ten, and drew one in Britain and played and won all four in France. It was some record to be proud of. My old adversary, Colin Meads, played a leading role in their triumphs and added to the controversial content by being sent off against Scotland at Murrayfield by Irish referee Kevin Kelleher.

With the All Blacks having come and gone, the domestic championship was not disrupted as the foot and mouth disease receded in Britain. Once more we lost to France in Paris but this game still evokes fond memories for me as it signalled the return to the Irish side after four years' absence of Syd Millar. I have referred elsewhere to the mystery of his absence for so long, but he proved his worthiness to be back for he was one who played extremely well that day in Paris.

Yet some good things were at hand, though once more England performed grand larceny by stealing a draw against us at Twickenham. That was the afternoon Bob Hiller made his debut for England at full-back and started on his personal conquest of Ireland. He kicked a magnificent penalty goal in the dying seconds to get England a draw. He kicked the goal from the right hand touchline after the referee, Merion Joseph of Wales, decreed that Brendan Sherry had deliberately thrown the ball into touch. Sherry strenuously denies to this day that he did so, but the referee's word is final and Hiller's right boot proved crucial.

That draw once again cost Ireland a Triple crown for we beat Scotland and Wales in Dublin. France won the championship and Ireland finished second.

The Lions were due to go to South Africa that summer and once more there was great speculation about who would lead the team. For my part, I felt Tom Kiernan was the obvious choice and the honour eventually went to him. David Brooks was appointed manager while for the first time the Lions had an official coach and there could have been no more appropriate choice for the job than Ronnie Dawson. The team contained some seasoned performers, several like myself who had been to New Zealand in 1966, and some great young players who had come on the international scene recently. Foremost in this respect were the young Welsh half-backs Gareth Edwards and Barry John, and threequarter Gerald Davies. They were not to leave a profound impact on the South African scene in that tour, but later their deeds would come out from the pages of rugby history.

When the historians come to look at the Lions tour of South Africa in 1968, they may decide that it followed a familiar pattern. Once more the Test series was lost and in the end decisively enough, by 3-0 with one match drawn. The thorough researcher will, on closer inspection, however, find that in fact only four out of twenty games were lost and that fifteen were won. The Lions scored 37 points. Those statistics will never reveal the full extent of what this tour achieved. For here was the turning point for rugby in Britain and Ireland and Dawson, Brooks and Kiernan deserve the utmost credit.

Initially I must say that it was a much better side than the test match results will convey. That apart, however, it brought home at last in the most effective manner possible what exactly was required if we were to match the Springboks and All Blacks on their own soil. Dawson and Brooks, to their ever-lasting credit, sought no refuge in hard luck, though the 1968 Lions suffered more than their share of it in many respects, injuries and bad refereeing being two prime causes.

On return home after the tour, Dawson and Brooks conveyed the message to the appropriate authorities that either we took the right road, reassessed our methods, paid proper attention to coaching at all levels of the game, or we would be better off resigning ourselves to the perennial role of good losers. They were not content with the rating, especially when they knew we had the players to do the job, all we needed was the coaching. No one could argue that even had we been free from injuries, we would have won the Test series, but I am confident we would have shared it.

Despite very limited opportunity and facilities, it was clear from the outset that Dawson and Brooks had put a lot of work into preparation; Dawson in particular was meticulous, much the more serious of the two men who were complementary one to the other. Brooks might have appeared to some to be too much one of the boys on the tour and not enough the manager, yet basically that would be a rash judgement. This was a happy tour from start to finish. Kiernan did a magnificent job in uniting the players, and at no stage on the tour, even when we knew we had lost the Test series, was there a division within the party nor were any players made feel that they were there for the Wednesday games.

We got off to a tremendous start and won the first six games of the tour. The seventh match was the first Test at Pretoria and that game was to inflict wounds that could never quite be healed. Barry John broke his collar-bone in the match and for almost a quarter of an hour we played with fourteen men even though by this time substitutes were allowed, the International Board having at its meeting that year ruled that injured players could be replaced in international games and games involving touring teams. Mike Gibson replaced John eventually but the Springboks won by 25 points to 20.

If we had got the impression during the run-up to the Test that provincial rugby in South Africa was not now quite so efficient as in the past, the Springboks left no doubt at all that they could still field a Test side of immense strength and their forward play had not diminished. The power and efficiency was still there in the persons of Marais, Pitzer, Myburgh, Du Preez, Jan Ellis and Tommy Bedford who was well versed in the ways of British rugby after a spell with Oxford University. Dawie de Villiers was now leading the side from scrum-half and he and Pete Visagie formed a very formidable half-back pairing.

Having struck the great psychological blow of winning the first Test, the Springboks were in the driving seat. Although we lost the provincial game immediately preceding the second Test against Transvaal, our only provincial defeat on the tour, we kept our hopes of keeping the series alive when we got a 6-6 draw in the second Test at Port Elizabeth.

It was not a great game by any means, each side scoring two penalty goals, but we got a sample in that game of unsatisfactory refereeing. The incident that led to us being awarded our second penalty, from which Kiernan kicked us level in the second half, emphasises the point. Mike Gibson was knocked cold by a deliberate punch. The referee obviously saw the infringement for he awarded a penalty, but if memory serves me correctly, that was the full extent of the action he took.

We went into the third Test at Cape Town knowing we had to win the game. Once more the spectre of injury hung over us. Gareth Edwards was now out and on that tour serious injury followed serious injury. John, Edwards, Keith Jarrett, Billy Raybould, all suffered major injuries, while Ken Goodall, who had come out as a replacement, managed to play only one match. It was that kind of misfortune which I believe ruined our chances of sharing the Test series.

We lost all hope of winning it when South Africa won the

third Test by 11-6. We were level at the interval, but then made a mistake immediately after the break and the Springboks got a try and seized the initiative. Kiernan again scored our 6 points and in the match immediately after the Test his understudy at full-back, Bob Hiller, kicked 23 points in helping us to a 26-6 win over Border in East London. Hiller eventually emerged as the leading points scorer on the tour even though he did not play in a Test.

Kiernan however kicked the 6 points we scored in losing 19-6 in the final Test, a game we had to play without having Edwards, John, Gerald Davies, Keri Jones and Mike Coulman available for selection. Kiernan had thus accounted for 35 of our 38 points in the series and that was a record for any player at that time in a Test series in South Africa. For the record, I got the other three points we scored in the series, a try in the first Test, so there was a distinct touch of green about the scoring in the series. Unfortunately though, it was not enough.

The tour was an extremely happy experience for me personally and it was to have profound influences on future events. I would be back in South Africa again, though I did not know that when we left Jan Smuts Airport for home at the end of July.

9
The History Makers

DESPITE the loss of the Test series in South Africa, an immense amount of good came out of the tour. There was certainly a new appreciation and a new awareness among most rugby legislators in the home countries.

Wales set the trend on the home front when they appointed a coach to their national side; the appointment had in fact been made before the 1968 tour when David Nash was put in charge of their national team. As yet we in Ireland had not come round to such a move but it could not be long delayed. When the 1969 championship got under way, however, the Irish Rugby Football Union had still not appointed a coach to the national side and the way things went initially for Ireland, some people thought such a step was hardly necessary.

The Australians came to Ireland on a short tour in the autumn of 1968 and we beat them at Lansdowne Road, our third win over Australia in two years. That game was in fact historic for it was the first international played under the new law which restricted kicking direct to touch between the 25 yard lines. It was not in fact a good advertisement for so revolutionary a step as the match was a poor one.

When we faced France in the first championship game in January 1969, we did so without the services of Mike Gibson, who had fractured his jaw in the final trial. His absence was in fact to prove very significant not alone for his future but for that of a young out-half who came for his first cap, Barry McGann.

I had never played on a winning team against France;

that afternoon I ended the dismal record for we won by 17 points to 9 and McGann, then a member of the Lansdowne club but more closely associated with Cork Constitution, made a great debut. The match also proved a personal triumph for our left wing, John Moroney, who scored 14 points, an Irish record, and as he was normally an out-half, 14 points playing out of position was some achievement.

We beat England by two points in the next game and this time Gibson was back and playing in the centre. We then went to Murrayfield and proved far too strong for Scotland, winning by 16 points to nil.

So the Triple Crown was at stake when we met Wales in Cardiff in March, as Wales had already beaten England and Scotland. It was a strange match played against a strange background. There was a major reconstruction job being done on the Arms Park and the capacity of the ground was reduced to around 30,000. The build-up to the game was intense, far too intense, and we went into the encounter without Ken Goodall, injured against Scotland and replaced by Mick Hipwell, who had made a return to international rugby after six years in the wilderness.

From the moment we arrived in Wales, it was obvious that there were many preconceived ideas about our play and how best to deal with it. Most of the ideas were wrong. We had been penalised a lot during the championship at the line-out for infringements at the rear of the line, a law that has since been amended. There were some in Wales who seemed to equate these penalties with robust play, yet throughout the series, not once had any of our players been penalised for anything other than technical infringements, indeed we had suffered quite a lot from injuries to our players during the series.

From the outset the match was full of tension and it was only ten minutes old when an incident, involving our flanker Noel Murphy and Brian Price, ended with Murphy on the ground, the recipient of a punch from Price delivered in full view of the referee. A lot has been written about the incident

77

and some have expressed the view, notably in Wales, that Murphy had been the aggressor in a ruck and that Price merely retaliated. But that is an unacceptable explanation. Price may well have been provoked verbally from the start of the game and lost his head, he most certainly was not struck by Noel Murphy or any other Irish player.

From that moment on, we seemed to lose concentration and there was a further outbreak of flying fists and once more another Irish player ended up on his back. It was an unedifying spectacle, but I can personally vouch for the fact that Ireland did not go on to the field with any intentions of doing other than playing rugby, while our captain Tom Kiernan was explicit in his command after the Price incident that we were not to retaliate.

Wales won the game and deserved to do so; that afternoon gave notice that they were going to be a power for a long time to come. Their full-back J. P. R. Williams was magnificent, and it was obvious that here was a player of exceptional quality as he was to prove later.

So we left Cardiff once more without the Triple Crown and the whole affair did little for the good name of rugby football, which was a pity as this was a truly great Welsh side. That defeat brought to an end a run of six consecutive wins for Ireland and if we achieved no crown or championship that season, we had by winning six matches on the trot, done something no other Irish side had managed.

By the start of the following season, there had been a very significant development when Ronnie Dawson was appointed coach to the team. Our first game under his leadership was against South Africa in January 1970 and we drew 8-8, thanks to a late penalty by Tom Kiernan when South Africa conceded a free under their own posts after a breakaway. A draw was a fair result to what was not a particularly good game.

That Springboks tour was notable above all else for demonstrations against apartheid. Some of the demonstrators went too far in their urgings to others not to attend matches against the Springboks, while for the South African players, it was an uncomfortable and an unhappy tour. I would never deny any person the right to demonstrate peacefully, but I certainly do deny the right of any demonstrator to intimidate visiting players or spectators who want to attend games and there was intimidation of spectators on this tour and incidents, notably in Scotland and Wales, in which several people were hurt. It was rather a contradiction that people were demonstrating against the intolerance and evils of apartheid and at the same time revealing their own intolerance; two voices, so to speak.

The Springboks found a vastly different approach to games in Britain and Ireland than any of their predecessors. They were sampling what it was to meet provincial and national teams that had undergone preparation. Now there were fewer mistakes to capitalise on and they found their own errors being punished more frequently. They had too a lot of problems from injuries. Yet they still had great players at their disposal in a side led by Dawi De Villiers. What was significant, however, was that they failed to beat any of the home countries. They drew with Wales and Ireland and lost to England and Scotland. Things were on the move at home.

Ireland lost to France and England in 1970, with Hiller again the match winner against us at Twickenham where he dropped two incredible goals in England's 9-3 win. But we beat Scotland in Dublin. So we faced Wales as rank outsiders in Dublin, a Welsh team in full cry for the Tripe Crown.

Not often in my international career have I played in an Irish side more determined to do well than the team that lined out against Wales that March day in 1970 at Lansdowne Road. We had a lot of experience in our side. Kiernan was still full-back and captain, Gibson was in the centre with Bresnihan, and Duggan and the Malone man, Bill Browne, were on the wings. McGann and Young formed a good half-back partnership while in the pack, Millar, Kennedy and Phil O'Callaghan were in front of Mick Molloy and myself and we had a great back row of Goodall, Fergus Slattery, who had made his debut against South Africa, and Ronnie Lamont, who had made a come-back after suffering an arm injury that had threatened to end his career.

We hammered Wales that afternoon, by 14 points to nil, a Welsh team that included Edwards and Barry John at half-back. J. P. R. Williams, Gerald Davies and Stewart Watkins were all on hand and a mighty pack that included most of those who had beaten us the previous year. The match was scoreless at the interval and then we took Wales apart in the second period with a display of sustained power and control forward, and tremendous application behind the scrum. Goodall was superb and scored a try to remember. Sadly it was his last game for Ireland as he turned professional that summer. It was also Syd Millar's last international, but there could not have been a better way to go out.

Ireland went to the Argentine that summer but it was an unsatisfactory tour from every possible viewpoint. We were short several players, including Gibson, and the itinerary of the tour left us in Buenos Aires for almost the complete stay. Furthermore we made the tour after a summer break. The best one can say about the two Tests is that they were torrid affairs with far too much emphasis on the physical. Both sides had players sent off in the first Test. Once more there was a great deal of dissatisfaction with law interpretation. I have no doubt had we travelled at a different time and with a full strength side (we were short Ken Kennedy, Roger Young, Fergus Slattery and a few others in addition to Gibson) things might have been very different. Yet it was clear that the Argentinians were learning rapidly.

The most unsavoury aspect of the tour came on the way home when we were ordered off the plane at Rio de Janeiro. To this day I never know why. We were all awaiting take-off for home, when, after a long delay, we were told to get off the plane and we did so. It was allegedly for bad behaviour, but the truth was that the airline had clearly overbooked the flight and the easy way out was to get rid of the Irish party. Several of the players had taken sleeping tablets in an effort to get a restful flight, and with a facility for perverting the truth, the Brazilian authorities and their press told the world we were everything from drunk to drugged. The party eventually got back home, some however had to wait several days in Rio.

The coming season, 1971, was an important one on the home front for this was another Lions tour year with New Zealand on the agenda in the summer. It proved to be Wales' year yet again and they won the Crown and Championship and did the grand-slam into the bargain. We had a reasonable year, notable for the return to the international scene of Ray McLoughlin after five years' absence and the international debut of tight head prop, Sean Lynch of St Mary's College, and his clubmate Denis Hickie, who had been on tour in Australia in 1967 but still awaited his first cap. We drew with France in Dublin and that game looked like the end of Tom Kiernan's career for he broke a bone in a leg and took no further part in rugby for the season. His replacement was Barry O'Driscoll who had been his understudy for some time.

We lost to England in Dublin, Mr Hiller again being the arch villian as far as we were concerned, kicking three penalty goals to our two tries. The try still had a value of only three points, but was shortly to be elevated to the more realistic value of four. We beat Scotland easily in Murrayfield, but once more Wales proved too strong at Cardiff.

In view of their performances and the quality of their players it was confidently expected that Wales would have the major representation on the Lions tour. Expectations were fully realised. Twelve months before the tour, the four Home Unions had announced that Doug Smith (Scotland) and Carwyn James (Wales) would be manager and coach respectively. The appointment of John Dawes, who had led Wales brilliantly to the grand-slam as Lions captain, was absolutely predictable and absolutely right. Dawes had the majority of his Welsh colleagues in the party and I was fortunate to be chosen along with Irish colleagues, Sean Lynch, Ray McLoughlin, Mick Hipwell, Fergus Slattery and Ireland's only representative behind the scrum, Mike Gibson.

There were four Scottish forwards in the party, Ian

81

McLauchlan, Sandy Carmichael, Gordon Brown and hooker Frank Laidlaw, while like Ireland, they had one back, Alistair Biggar. England supplied hooker John Pullin, back row Peter Dixon, then uncapped, and behind the scrum, David Duckham, Bob Hiller, Chris Wardlow and John Spencer. But it was Wales who provided the hard core of the party; J. P. R. Williams, John Bevan, Gerald Davies, Barry John, Gareth Edwards, Chico Hopkins, Arthur Lewis, and the general himself, John Dawes, among the backs, and Delme Thomas, Mike Roberts, John Taylor, Derek Quinnell and Mervyn Davies in the forwards, a total of 13 players in all.

There was talent and skill among that touring party; great strength forward, flair and brilliance behind the scrum. It was obvious from the moment the party assembled that Carwyn James and Doug Smith were a complementary pair and had a tremendous relationship with the players and understanding of them. In Dawes we had the ideal players' representative.

More wordage has been poured out about the 1971 New Zealand tour than any other in history. I want to consider it from a player's viewpoint however and I want especially to recall the contributions made by Carwyn James, Doug Smith, John Dawes and Ray McLoughlin. McLoughlin did not play in a Test because he had been injured in an infamous match at Canterbury, the ninth of the tour in New Zealand. I have no hesitation in saying that the approach of the Canterbury players in that match did no credit to the team that at the time were the New Zealand champions, Ranfurly Shield holders. They approached the game with a win-at-all-costs attitude and while they did not achieve their objective of winning—we beat them 14-3—they played in a manner that took a frightful toll on the Lions. There is a famous photograph of Sandy Carmichael after he received an injury to his face. It was in fact a multiple fracture of the cheek-bone, the product of what I can only describe as a vicious assault. Mick Hipwell, John Dawes, John Pullin and Gareth Edwards were all injured in the game and the referee in that match had no reason to feel pleased that he did not follow the law book, for how he tolerated some of the brutality that went on is difficult to fathom. As events transpired, Hipwell, Carmichael and Ray McLoughlin did not play again on tour. McLoughlin broke a bone in a hand during the game. But I run ahead of my time, for I want to get back to the build-up for the tour and the work put in on it by what I will call the management.

From the moment we assembled at Eastbourne to prepare before the journey to Australia, it was plain that James, Smith and Dawes believed that we could win the Test series. They transmitted that confidence to the whole playing party. It was obvious that Smith and James had done their homework down to the most minute detail. I remember before the team was picked being approached by the two men and asked about New Zealand and what kind of players I thought would be suitable. I do not know whether they heeded my advice, but they sought it and that was typical of the men and their attitude, and it never varied from start to finish of that great tour.

Carwyn James had time for everybody. His is not alone a fine rugby mind, he is also a great psychologist. He knew the personalities of every player and he knew how to deal with every player in every circumstance. I have not come across a better combination in the art of man-management than the manager and coach of the 1971 Lions. James would seek everyone's point of view and listened to it with respect. Doubtless he did what he thought best, irrespective of advice offered to him, but you left him feeling here is a man who respects me and wants to hear what I think. His analysis of opponents was nothing short of brilliant and his reading of the game astonishing.

Doug Smith had that great facility for gaining respect without the use of the heavy hand and at no time on the tour did he make a wrong move. That is the best tribute I can pay to the man I would unhesitatingly name as the greatest manager under whom it was my privilege to play. Quite apart from his qualities of leadership, Dawes was a great player, yet he was the most underrated of my era. He was not a flamboyant centre, but none did the basics better than Dawes. His passing was perfect; he always did the right thing at the right time and his leadership was nothing less than superb.

I bracket Ray McLoughlin with the management trio because although he did not play in a Test, his contribution was immense. He did a great deal of coaching on the forwards and I remember in particular one stage of the tour when he set about building up our physical strength. 'They are supposed to be physically stronger than us,' he told the players, 'so we will get stronger.' He was as good as his word.

When we lost the first of our two games in Australia against Queensland, the knockers were in quickly to say that for all our preparations we had hardly shown that we were going to do any better than some of our predecessors. It was a rash judgement as things turned out. We beat New South Wales in the second game and then it was on to New Zealand.

We reached the first Test in Dunedin with ten wins out of ten; the rugby world had by now sat up and taken notice. I shall not forget the build-up for the first Test and Carwyn's assessment of what he wanted from us. We did not let him down and won by 9 points to 3. It was the proverbial cliffhanger but a win of incalculable benefit.

In the early stages of that game, the All Blacks came on us in waves. Gareth Edwards went into the game with a hamstring injury and had to be replaced by Chico Hopkins after ten minutes; and how well the Llanelli man played when his hour came! We led 4-3 at half-time, Ian McLauchlan got a try for us after charging down an attempted clearance. Fergie McCormack kicked a penalty for the All Blacks and then in the second half Barry John kicked two penalty goals and we were home. McLauchlan and Sean Lynch were the props that afternoon and were to be together in all four Tests. It was during the tour that the diminutive Scot earned the title 'Mighty Mouse' for his exploits. Mighty he was, but no mouse; a Lion in every sense of the word if not in stature, his heart provided all that was required to meet the physical demands.

John's two penalty goals were just two of the many great

and invaluable scores he got on the tour and the title 'King John' that he earned was a title of which he was worthy. But he was just one of a great bunch of players.

We might have lost that first Test, but we did not. This time we were able to stand up to the pressures put on us by the All Blacks. It was not until three minutes from time that John sealed it for us with his second penalty. We had matched them forward and we knew we were better than them behind the scrum. Events were to prove that assessment to be right. Colin Meads who had led the All Blacks that day was gracious enough when it was all over to say, 'The better team won on the day'. Maybe only just better, but we were better nevertheless.

I shall never forget how I felt after that match; I have seldom known a prouder moment in my life. I had endured the humiliations of 1966, so to win a Test in New Zealand gave me indescribable pleasure. Now we knew Carwyn was right, we really could take this series, but it would be a long, hard road.

The victory march continued, that is until the second Test and we were beaten comprehensively in that game at Christchurch. So the roaring Lions had been silenced at last. New Zealand was not going to bend the knee to this side. We were going to earn a Test victory the hard way. Fears that we might have suffered an irreversible blow by that loss in the second Test were soon dispelled by Carwyn who now had to work without Ray McLoughlin's assistance for he had gone home as had Mick Hipwell. Stack Stevens of England and Trevor Evans of Wales came out as replacements.

We won all the games between the second and third Tests and we knew when we took the field at Wellington that we faced the big crunch in the series. We had to win this one if we were going to take the series. And we did in the end, by 13 points to 3. Fergus Slattery was selected for this game, but he was unable to play and we went into the game with an all Welsh back row of Derek Quinnell, Mervyn Davies and John Taylor. They played brilliantly in cutting off the threat of All Blacks scrum-half, Sid Going, who had done immense damage to us in the second Test.

We won the third Test in twenty minutes of rugby for we were 13 points up in that time. John struck the first blow with a dropped goal and then he converted a try by Gerald Davies from the touchline. They would never forget him in New Zealand for he teased and tantalised more opposing full-backs in particular, and opponents in general, on that tour than I can aptly describe. He had able assistants, notably the best scrum-half in the world and a threequarter line of sheer brilliance in Davies, Duckham, Gibson and Dawes and a full-back in J. P. R. Williams who assumed the stature of a world class player in New Zealand and has if anything improved on it in the intervening period of time.

John it was who contributed the other five points to our total when he scored a try near the posts and converted it. We would not be caught now and we were not. But it was not easy, for the All Blacks came at us, but once more we matched them, while Gibson in particular was magnificent in countering their attempts to break through behind the scrum. So now all we wanted in the final Test was a draw. I think everyone in New Zealand wanted to be at the game in Auckland.

I have often been asked if we went out to play for a draw in that game and the answer is firmly in the negative. Such a policy would have been ridiculous against a side of the All Blacks calibre. As things turned out, it ended in a draw, but that sufficed for our needs and when it was all over, Colin Meads made the prediction that no side would ever again beat the All Blacks in a Test series on their own ground. I wonder if time will prove him right? We did it and so history was made. We became the first Lions side to win a Test series in New Zealand and that amounted to what many believed was impossible. The match was a draw at 14 points all.

We knew that afternoon before we went out what we were likely to face. This was New Zealand with backs to the wall. They had to win. They were desperate and that ring of desperation cost them their chance of victory for they conceded some needless penalty kicks, notably three by the same player, who thought his brief was to kick every Lion he saw on the ground. Not all his team-mates followed a similar policy fortunately for the good of our health and the welfare of the game.

We were five points down after three minutes, and eight down after just thirteen minutes. Then John kicked a penalty for us to give us renewed hope. Despite the deficit, I never felt we were going to be engulfed. The forwards were hardened now and able to match the All Blacks physically and technically. We were level by half-time when Peter Dixon got a try which John converted, and just after the interval we went ahead for the first time when John kicked a 40 yards penalty goal. They equalised with a try and then J. P. R. Williams dropped a great goal to put us ahead at 14-11. Gordon Brown who had been the target for more than a little rough treatment, had to go off injured and was replaced by Delme Thomas. The All Blacks equalised with a penalty, but could do no more and when the final whistle went, we had done it, beaten the All Blacks on their own soil. Doug Smith's prediction at the start of the tour that we would take the series, by winning two and drawing one of the four Tests had come true to the last letter. He admitted afterwards that he had made that prediction with tongue in cheek. But he believed we would win and he was right.

Why did we win? Had rugby gone down in New Zealand rather than up in Britain and Ireland? We won because of discipline, dedication, flair, commitment and magnificent management. We won because we were able to equal the All Blacks forward, something that had not happened previously and we beat them behind the scrum. At no stage would I say we dominated the All Blacks pack. But it was not a case of rugby deteriorating in New Zealand, rather a new era dawning in Britain and Ireland. Coaching, team-work and the ability to utilise the talents that flow from those attributes had done the trick.

I like to think that win in New Zealand provided a tremendous impetus for the game in the home countries and I firmly believe that such was the case. There was above all tremendous character in that 1971 Lions side. The conservatives at home who had decried coaching were routed. The progressives had won, and in James, Smith and Dawes, the progressives could not have had more worthy representatives. In the Lions squad, the management could not have had more dedicated players who came back with a record that read : Played 26; won 24; drew 1; lost 2; points for 580; points against 231, and one of those defeats had been inflicted in Australia in the first game of the tour. Barry John topped the scoring list with 191. Long live the King!

10
Commander of Dad's Army

T H E victory of the Lions in New Zealand had a great influence for good on the game in Britain and Ireland. The Welsh contribution to the success had been immense and it was not surprising that they were the firm favourites to win the Championship in the 1972 season. They had, for instance, J. P. R. Williams at full-back, Gerald Davies on one wing, Barry John and Gareth Edwards at half-back, and a hard core of experienced and talented forwards around which to build a really formidable pack.

Yet I thought Ireland had chances in 1972. Tom Kiernan had made a great recovery from the leg injury which had at one time threatened to end his career. Mike Gibson's performances in New Zealand had underlined the fact that he was playing better than ever and Barry McGann was an experienced out-half who had been on the Irish side since 1969. We did however appear to have problems behind the scrum, but they were solved by shrewd selection.

In the pack, we had what I believed to be the best front row in the game, Ray McLoughlin, Ken Kennedy and Sean Lynch; while Denis Hickie, who had come into the side with great success at number eight in 1971 was playing extremely well and Fergus Slattery must by now have been an even better player than he was when selected for the Lions.

The Interprovincial Championship in Ireland is often subjected to severe criticism, but I think it is the best system that we could have for vetting prospective candidates for the Irish side each year. For one thing, it is competitive, the essential element so often missing in trial games. That year, it provided enough information for the Irish selectors. Leinster won the championship and had surprised many by recalling Kevin Flynn in the centre. Kevin had been a great centre for Ireland between 1959 and 1966 and had had more than his share of injuries. He fell out of the representative scene, but his form for his club, Wanderers, was deeply impressive that season.

His performances for Leinster were good enough at any rate to win him recognition on the Irish side for the game against France in Paris where Ireland had not won for twenty-one years and where I had never played on a winning team. The inclusion of Flynn certainly upped the age ratio of the Irish side at a time when many believed that it should be coming down. 'Old soldiers', wrote one critic, 'do not fade away from the Irish side, they make come-backs. Flynn added experience to the Irish side, but an infusion of young blood might have been a wiser policy.' Flynn was, admittedly over thirty, but he was still a class player and had proved himself better than any of the contenders as Gibson's midfield partner.

Nor could the accusation of not bringing in youngsters really be sustained. We went to Paris with five new caps in the side. Tom Grace, a big strong running wing from U.C.D. was on the right wing and my Ballymena clubmate Wallace McMaster was on the left, and at scrum-half John Moloney, of St Mary's College, who had toured with Ireland in the Argentine came in for Roger Young, now out of the representative scene to concentrate on his dental practice.

In the pack, Con Feighery of Lansdowne was brought in as my second row partner and Dungannon flanker Stewart McKinney, a strong and durable player (but vastly under-rated by many), seemed at the time a very wise selection. He would be the ideal partner for Slattery; his strength, courage and ability to tidy up in ruck, maul and at the back of the line-out was a special requirement against the French.

Ireland won a great victory at Colombes by 14 points to 9. We led by 11-3 at half-time and were well worth the lead. The surprising thing about that first half and the advantage we built up was not the lead but the fact that Ray McLoughlin scored a try, an unusual occurrence to say the least. The score epitomised McLoughlin's incredible strength when he broke from a maul about ten yards from the French line and drove forward. I told him if he fancied himself as a runner with the ball the best place for him was the threequarter line. We did not want youngsters like him showing up our lack of pace. Ray greeted his try as if it were an everyday happening, which I hastened to point out it was not. I told him I could not remember him scoring a try before, but he assured me that was because of a bad memory.

We played exceptionally well in Paris and Tom Kiernan added a second penalty goal to one he had scored in the first half; Moloney had scored a try after about eight minutes, a great start to his international career. France did get a late try by Lux and that great full-back Pierre Villepreux converted, but we were in command and had no real problems holding off the French.

The next match was also an away game, against England at Twickenham. We had won only once there in my time, in 1964 when Mike Gibson made such a sensational debut and that win, eight years previously, was Ireland's only success at Twickenham in a period of nearly twenty-five years, the great Triple Crown team of 1948 had also been successful at the venue. It was in fact an unlucky ground for us. I found it difficult to understand an attitude in the game by some people who thought a match at Twickenham was rather easier than in Paris, Cardiff or Murrayfield. The atmosphere is different, the supporters more reserved than at Cardiff, Dublin and Paris, but one never got anything easy from England at Twickenham.

We went there with an unchanged side, not surprising in view of our win in Paris. Once more it was proved just how difficult England could be to overcome, especially with Bob Hiller in their team. Not since Oliver Cromwell can an Englishman have inflicted such hardship on the Irish as did Hiller. He had beaten us in Dublin the previous year by kicking three penalty goals. In 1970, he dropped two incredible goals to win the match for England and in 1969 in Dublin all but did the damage once more when he kicked four penalty goals. But it was in 1968 that he committed his great act of grand larceny when he landed a penalty goal from the right hand touchline in injury time to give England a 9-9 draw. Hiller was again in the England side in 1972, as captain.

We had come away from Twickenham so many times as losers in games that we should have won, that it was time luck fell our way. It did so on 12 February 1972. Hiller had been up to his tricks again. He had kicked a penalty goal and converted a try by Chris Ralston to give England a 9-3 lead at half-time. Tom Grace scored a try for Ireland, Hiller kicked a penalty for England and Barry McGann dropped a goal for Ireland, but it did seem enough. With the game well into injury time, England were leading 12-10 when we won a scrum near their '25'. Moloney threw a beautiful pass to McGann who sent Kevin Flynn on his way and the 'old man' with a classic break split the England defence to score near the posts. Kiernan converted but it did not matter. We had robbed England this time—poetic justice. Ironically, Hiller was dropped from the England side after that game and then retired from international rugby. So we had seen him off, but I was sorry to see Bob go, he was a great team-mate on the Lions tours of 1968 and 1971 and a fine full-back. I must say, however, that I was relieved when subsequently I played against England to find that Hiller was not in the side.

So we had won two games away from home and now faced the prospect of meeting Scotland and Wales in Dublin. A Triple Crown? A Championship? Well, who could blame us for thinking in those terms. Then politics took a hand. The troubles in Northern Ireland took on a new meaning in the world of rugby when it was announced that Scotland had refused to travel to play us in Dublin. Admittedly the British Embassy had been burned down in the aftermath of what has become known as 'Bloody Sunday' in Derry when thirteen civilians were shot dead in incidents with the British Army. It was announced by the Scottish Rugby Union that they were not prepared to send a team to Dublin out of consideration for their players and supporters. A delegation from the Irish Rugby Union travelled to Edinburgh to try and get Scotland to come, but it was to no avail.

The Welsh Rugby Union followed the lead given by the Scots. Alternative venues were offered to the Irish, but to their everlasting credit, the I.R.F.U. refused to play the games anywhere but Lansdowne Road.

The events surrounding the cancellations of these matches have been documented well enough to make it unnecessary for me to go into all the sordid details. I must say, however, that I found it hard to understand the attitude of the Scots and the Welsh, especially in view of the overtures made to them by a collection of eminent men whose assurances and first-hand knowledge of the situation in Ireland were rejected.

The Irish team was bitterly disappointed, and having discussed the matter with many of the Scots and Welsh players subsequently, I know that they too were disappointed. In some instances at least, the feeling was one of disagreement with the decisions taken by their administrators.

One of the unfortunate aspects of the whole affair was the amount of ill-informed comment made by sections of the British press. They wrote about the cancellations from points well removed from the scene and some of the material they produced was utterly imaginative, certainly not based on fact. Not all the British rugby writers followed such a line, but those cancellations were to have an echo twelve months later when England were due to visit Dublin. So no crown, no championship for Ireland, or indeed for anyone else; and Wales and Ireland ended the season unbeaten. France agreed to come to Ireland and play a match in Dublin, a great gesture by the French and one that helped ease the financial burden imposed by the cancellation of two internationals, certain to draw capacity attendances to Lansdowne Road.

It will always be a matter for speculation as to whether or not Ireland would have beaten Scotland and Wales, but those who claimed that Wales had in essence won the title because they beat France, England and Scotland, did Ireland less than justice. We had beaten Wales in Dublin by 14 points in 1970 and I think that the Irish side of 1972 was one of the best if not the best I played in. There was great strength forward, experience and skill behind the scrum. Players such as Ray McLoughlin, Ken Kennedy, Sean Lynch, Fergus Slattery, Mike Gibson, Barry McGann, Kevin Flynn and Tom Kiernan were still as good as ever and in some respects better.

We got some measure of compensation, however, when France came to Dublin, were given a great reception and a good beating into the bargain by the Irish side to which wing Alan Duggan returned as replacement for the injured Tom Grace and Mick Hipwell came in at number eight for Denis Hickie who was also injured. We won by 24 points to 14, but what was more important was the proof that internationals could take place in Dublin without hinderance or trouble of any kind, something that we had known all the time.

The All Blacks were scheduled to come to Ireland in 1972-73, and their visit is always an auspicious occasion for the game in the home countries. Following their defeat in the Test series, there was, of course, much speculation on the composition of the tourists' party and its strength. I think the results of the tour indicated that New Zealand had not yet recovered from the Lions achievements and that replacing men such as Colin Meads, my old adversary and friend, and Brian Lochore, to mention just two, was not going to be easy and needed time and patience.

From the moment the team; captained by flanker Ian Kirkpatrick, arrived in Britain—in fact at the first press conference given by them in London—the question of the Irish part of the tour was raised. Would they be prepared to travel to Belfast, for instance, in view of the civil unrest in the North of Ireland? Would they go to Dublin? Were they aware that Wales and Scotland had refused to play in Dublin some months previously? Tour manager Ernie Todd told the world that it was their intention to play every fixture on their itinerary and that they were prepared to take the advice of people whom they considered qualified to give it. In the case of Ireland that meant the security forces and the Irish Rugby Football Union. Mr Todd, who died in 1975 after a long illness, was as good as his word. The All Blacks came to Ireland, not once but twice. They got a great reception in Belfast and I think enjoyed their visit to Ulster to which they were prepared to come, unlike some others whose association with Ulster was supposed to be so close for so long, but who steadfastly refused to play at Ravenhill. It mattered little that the All Blacks beat Ulster, mattered little in the broad context that is, but it was vitally important that the game was played.

Munster, in their traditional manner, gave the tourists a great game in Cork with New Zealand getting a penalty goal in injury time to save the game.

Four days later Ireland met them at Lansdowne Road and the result was a 10-10 draw. Tom Grace got a great try for Ireland near the end and Barry McGann's conversion attempt went about an inch wide of the near post, thus saving New Zealand's unbeaten record against Ireland. The match against New Zealand was Kevin Flynn's last for Ireland; he was replaced by the young Bangor player Dick Milliken, a solid and courageous centre with a lot of potential and I thought the ideal partner for Mike Gibson now that Kevin had gone. There were more than a few who thought it was time a few more of us went too, but the selectors did not see it that way.

The next match was against England in Dublin and once more the speculation began in the British press as to whether England would come. Vigorous attempts were made by two journalists in particular to stop England coming. 'Why', wrote one of them, 'should England players be subjected to playing on a ground enclosed in barbed wire and surrounded by armed police.' That statement did nothing but bring the press into disrepute, for no games in Dublin were played in such circumstances. The English selectors were advised that it would be grossly irresponsible of them to ask the players to travel to Dublin and 'risk life and limb'. But the English selectors and the Rugby union committee were made of sterner stuff and not influenced by the scare talk of two reporters and the general belief among the British press was that England should come.

The Rugby Union President, Dick Kingswell, announced that it was England's full intention to travel to Dublin and fulfil the fixture. There were suggestions that a few of the English players were not happy about travelling. I rang one or two of them and told them that they had nothing to fear by playing in Ireland; furthermore, Mr Kingswell and the chairman of the English selectors, Sandy Sanders, said that any player who did not want to travel was perfectly at liberty to inform them of his feelings and it would not in any way affect his selection for subsequent matches. But as far as I know, England were able to play the team they required and the selectors were not in any way impeded in their choice for the match. The reception England got that day in Dublin was one of the greatest moments in sporting history. I shall never forget it. For five minutes the crowd stood and applauded England. It was a tremendous triumph for rugby and for sport over politics and England rendered the game a service that afternoon which cannot easily be repaid. We beat them too—Hiller had gone by now—and that night at the dinner for the teams and officials, England captain John Pullin brought the house down when he said: We may not be the best team in the world, but we do turn up!

The next assignment was Scotland at Murrayfield, a game we lost and one that holds particularly sad memories for me. It was Tom Kiernan's last game for Ireland. Appropriately, he scored a try that day and one of his last acts on the international rugby field was to wave a hand in the air near the end of the match to signal a Scottish dropped goal 'good'. It was typical of the man.

Kiernan was dropped for the match against Wales in Cardiff and replaced by the young Wanderers player, Tony Ensor, and I was given the captaincy of Ireland. I was following a man who led his country on twenty-four occasions, and no player in rugby history has ever led his country more often

Relaxing with Gareth Edwards in South Africa during the 1974 tour.

'Mister Willie John McBride and the Lions pack . . . '
(The cartoonists had a field day at the end of the 1974 tour.)

COLORSPORT

In action against England at Twickenham. Chris
Rowleston and Andy Ripley in attendance.

THE ARGUS, CAPE TOWN

My 34th birthday party in Cape Town with John Williams, Ian McLauchlan,
Tom David, John Maloney and Bobby Windsor.

Leading out the Irish team against England at Twickenham,
16 February 1974. My fifty-sixth cap—a world record.

A busy weekend: scoring my first ever— and only—try for Ireland in the match against France at Lansdowne Road, 1 March 1975, and the next day addressing an interdenominational service for sportsmen and women in St Ann's Church, Dublin.

Sportsman of the Year 1974. Max Aiken, Chairman of Beaverbrook Newspapers, seems lost in contemplation!

DAILY EXPRESS

With Penny, Paul and Amanda holding Willie the Lion who accompanied me as mascot on the 1974 tour, arriving home at Belfast.

With Syd Millar in the Millar-McBride room at Ballymena.

The Ballymena 1st XV, 1974-75 winners of the Ulster Senior Cup.

than Kiernan. He had played fifty-four times for Ireland so he was dropped just one cap short of Colin Meads' world record of fifty-five caps for New Zealand. I suppose it proved a point that sentiment did not play a part in the selection of Irish teams, an accusation made first against the Irish selectors in the closing stages of Jackie Kyle's international career and repeated on subsequent occasions. I did not believe it then and I do not believe it now.

We lost to Wales in Cardiff by four points and after that game Barry McGann was omitted for the last match of the season, against France in Dublin. Mick Quinn of Lansdowne came into the side for McGann and he made a winning debut as we beat France by 6-4, a result that brought about an extraordinary end to the International Championship. It ended in a quintuple tie, all countries ending up with four points. It was the only time in history that such a thing had happened. So the countries shared the championship: it was suggested that we all also shared the wooden spoon, which was what we deserved after a poor season. I suppose it depended on what way you looked at it; championship or spoon, we shared them both really. It was better than finishing alone at the bottom anyway.

Kiernan could be said to have been the first of the old brigade to depart from the international scene. More than a few thought it was time that more of the 'Chelsea Pensioners' followed a similar path. We had quite a few who had seen their thirtieth birthdays, Ray McLaughlin and myself had celebrated them more than just a year or two earlier. Ken Kennedy, Mike Gibson, Sean Lynch were now all over the thirty mark. It was time for us to go before we were dispensed with. The front five on the Irish side consisted of four over-30's, a kind of geriatric unit. I think we were expected to take the field hobbling on our walking sticks. Certainly the age of the side gave rise to no little comment and I suppose it had to happen that someone thought up the 'ideal' title for Ireland — 'Dad's Army', after the popular television series based on the exploits of a battalion of the Home Guard.

So Dad's Army it was and I was again appointed to com-

G

mand. I accepted the role with great pride and no little hope. I thought we had a lot of skill at our disposal and if we could not run to the trenches as quickly as a year or two earlier, we were well able to defend them. We were not altogether short of ammunition either.

Kennedy was still the best technically-endowed hooker in the game and we had a few spring chickens among the old cocks in the pack who could move a bit too. My second row partner Moss Keane, a good subject of the Kingdom of Kerry, was like myself a farmer's son and his background was equally as unlikely as my own for a rugby international. However, unlike me, he had been a very proficient Gaelic footballer, good enough to have played at minor level for his native county which was its own recommendation in an area where Gaelic football is not so much a sport as a way of life. He had been introduced to rugby when he went to University College Cork, a university that had a rugby tradition dating back over 100 years and had given some great players to Ireland.

Moss, no more than McBride, did not signal his international debut with a win. We lost to France in Paris and were decidedly unlucky to lose, going down 9-6 in a game that had more than its share of the controversial, with Ireland being on the losing end of two decisions of that nature. Our battle was not over on the field either, for Moss and myself were almost arrested in Paris that night after we went into a cafe to buy something to eat. We were jostled by a few tough guys and, before we knew where we were, we seemed to be surrounded by an army—less friendly than Dad's though. But we managed to fight our way clear.

The next match was against Wales in Dublin, the first time we had met them at Lansdowne Road for four years. They came to Dublin for that match as warm favourites. Ireland had made two changes from the side that lost in Paris. Seamus Deering, a member of a great rugby family and a player whose father and uncle had played for Ireland came in on the flank for Stewart McKinney, while Pat Lavery of London

Irish was on the left wing as replacement for Wallace McMaster who was injured. For me the game was a very special occasion. Matches against Wales always were, but I had other reasons that afternoon as I played my fifty-fifth game for Ireland and so equalled Colin Meads' record. Ray McLoughlin said that it proved just how easy it was to play in the second row when two fellows like Meads and myself could play fifty-five times for our countries. 'Big and ignorant, that's all that's required', said Ray. Whatever the requirements, I was very proud when I led Ireland on to the field that day when the match ended in a 9-9 draw. It was not a quality performance from either side, certainly not in keeping with the vast amount of experience and skill contained in the two teams.

So for both Wales and ourselves there would now be no Triple Crown and having lost three out of four points in our first two matches, it seemed unlikely that Ireland would win the championship.

Syd Millar was now the Irish coach, he had taken over the previous season from Ronnie Dawson, whose contribution as the first man ever to hold down the position of coach to an Irish side had been so immense. I was more sorry for Dawson than anyone else when the 1972 campaign had ended in such unsatisfactory fashion with the cancellation of the matches against Wales and Scotland. But Dawson had proved beyond the bounds of reasonable argument just how beneficial it was to have a coach to the national team. In a later chapter I put forward more strenuous opinions in that direction.

Millar had taken over the job in rather controversial circumstances for he had retired as a player only a matter of months before he became Irish coach. And in fact he had been appointed coach to the Ulster team for the 1972-73 season, but of course had to relinquish that appointment when the Irish selectors named him as Dawson's successor. Millar felt that we had the beating of England and that was a view shared among the team. England had been tipped as the 'team of the year', following their astonishing feat of beating New Zealand on a short tour the previous summer. That win was all the more amazing as England had been due to travel to Argentina but cancelled the tour because of political unrest. They took the tour to New Zealand at the shortest possible notice and against the advice of many people who believed, and I must say with good reason, that a tour to New Zealand was extremely difficult in any circumstances, but without great preparation it was asking for trouble. Anyway, England went and made a great success of the venture.

Perhaps the most incredible thing about the tour was that England lost the three provincial games they played on it and yet won the only Test. England too had started the international campaign in 1974 by losing a remarkable match against Scotland at Murrayfield by 16 points to 14, with the Scots full-back, Andy Irvine, kicking the winning penalty in injury time. England had played well enough in that game to indicate that they had a lot of talent, even if they were prone to make mistakes in vital situations. Perhaps we could capitalise on such failings. The majority did not think so, for we made the journey to Twickenham as rank outsiders. The speed and agility of the England pack would see off Dad's Army, and with little trouble.

England had a strong looking pack. Fran Cotton, John Pullin and Stack Stevens were in the front row, Roger Uttley and Chris Ralston in the second row and Tony Neary and Peter Dixon were on the flanks with the flamboyant Andy Ripley at number eight. All of them were being widely tipped to make the Lions squad for the South African tour in the summer. Nor was all their strength in the pack, for David Duckham was on one wing, Alan Old at out-half, Geoff Evans in the centre and all three of them were deemed near certainties for the Lions tour too. We put a side in the field against them that had Tom Grace back on the right wing. He had surprisingly been dropped from the game against France and left out again against Wales in favour of the Lansdowne player Vinny Becker, an Irish sprint champion. McMaster was back on the left wing and Stewart McKinney had been restored on the flank.

We were quite content in the role of outsiders, the berth we fill so often in international rugby, but if this was, as the critics in general maintained, going to be England's year, it was Ireland's day at Twickenham on 16 February 1974.

We went to Twickenham looking for our third successive win over England and we got it by 26 points to 21. By scoring 26 points we equalled the highest total ever achieved by an Irish side. Only once previously had Ireland scored 26 points, against Scotland in 1953. So Dad's Army still had some fire power left and I will never subscribe to the view expressed after the match that we were hanging on at the finish.

True, at one time we were leading by 26 points to 9 and playing as well as any Irish team I had been in had ever played. Then Alan Old kicked England back into the match. He scored two penalty goals and converted a try to bring England within sight of us with ten minutes to go, but we finished strongly. Gibson scored two great tries that afternoon, Terry Moore, our big number eight and another who had made a come-back to international rugby the previous season, and John Moloney scored tries, Gibson converted two, Tony Ensor kicked a penalty goal and Mick Quinn, who had played splendidly at out-half, dropped a goal and played a major part in the construction of one of Gibson's tries.

Our last match was against Scotland in Dublin, and results in the series had taken a trend that gave us a chance of winning the championship provided things went well against the Scots and the remaining games in the championship series resulted in home wins.

I would like to make the point here that our win at Twickenham was the first by any country away from home for two years in the championship. Furthermore our victory over England at Twickenham in 1972 had been the last recorded by a country on opponents soil. I think that said something for the character of the Irish side of that era. It was by no means a team of all the talents, but it was a greatly under-rated side. The limited playing population in Ireland, especially compared with Wales, England and France, inevitably means that in at least a few places Ireland are invariably forced to compromise. In a word, it is difficult for us to field 15 international class players in 15 positions. I think it true to say that some players have got into Irish teams who might not have made the national teams of other countries, but the spirit and will often made up for other deficiencies. When one thinks for instance of the pick available to the English selectors and compares it to the position that obtains in Ireland, we have done remarkably well in international rugby and the period from 1968 to 1974 was one of great achievement, even if as yet a championship or Triple Crown had not been won.

We met Scotland on 2 March and won the match by 9 points to 6. That same afternoon England drew 12-12 with France in Paris, so the championship would now hinge on what happened on the last day of the series when France had to meet Scotland at Murrayfield and England were playing against Wales at Twickenham. Our win over Scotland left us with five points and at the top of the table. Both Wales and France would overhaul us if they won. If they both drew, then it would be a three-way tie at the top of the table between France, Wales and ourselves.

In some respects we were lucky to be in the position of still being able to win the championship for we had a ring of good fortune against the Scots in Dublin. We were 9 points up at half-time, with Dick Milliken having scored a try, Mike Gibson a conversion and Stewart McKinney kicked a penalty goal, his first attempt, incidentally, at a penalty for Ireland.

We had the wind at our backs in the first half, and an appreciable wind it was too. But we had more than held our own against the Scots pack that included Sandy Carmichael, Ian McLauchlan, and Gordon Brown, all three of whom had been with the Lions in New Zealand and had made major contributions to the success of that side. In addition, Scotland had a fine line-out player in Alistair McHarg, a man freely tipped to go to South Africa with the Lions in the coming summer.

The Scots' pack which had laboured a lot in the first period, began to win more possession, but their backs could not translate it into scores against a great Irish defence. We had one very narrow escape when Scotland almost got a try after a sweeping forward rush, but we cleared the danger and it was not until about a quarter of an hour from the end that we conceded a score and then it was a penalty goal kicked by the young Scottish full-back, Andy Irvine.

Gibson was outstanding among the Irish backs and one great interception brought us a lot of relief, but as time wore on, we gradually began to get to grips with the Scots up front again. Irvine kicked his second penalty with two minutes to go and that was not enough.

So we had won, but once more the cry went up that Ireland had faded in the second period. They were still anxious to open the gates of the geriatric unit for us oldtimers. I think that in many ways such an argument was unfair to the Scottish pack, who had come together in great fashion after getting a bit of a hammering in the first half. It was a case of Scotland playing much better after the interval than a fade-out by Ireland.

We had held the Welsh, beaten England, defeated Scotland, yet in some quarters all those results were greeted with marked scepticism. Whether or not we were now going to win the championship, at least we were assured that we would not finish in the place forecast for us, the bottom of the championship ladder. However profound our senility, however imminent our confinement to the wheelchairs, we were in with a chance of winning the championship even if events were outside our control.

There was more than just a little interest in Ireland at the happenings at Murrayfield and Twickenham on the afternoon of 16 March 1974. I was playing with my club, Ballymena, that afternoon, and when I came off the field, I was told that Scotland had beaten France easily at Murrayfield, and then came news that England, against all the predictions had beaten Wales at Twickenham. England could not have chosen a better occasion to gain their first win over Wales for eleven years and their first over the Welsh at Twickenham for fourteen years.

So Ireland were champions. 'The Luck of the Irish', went one newspaper heading, and that was true enough. Another, and from a not unexpected quarter read: 'Ireland are champions at last—by default'.

We had finished with five points and that was one more than Wales, France and Scotland, who by their win had come up into joint second place. England despite their win over Wales had to be content with the wooden spoon. So it was not after all to be England's but Ireland's year and it was truly great to be part of it. My only regret was that Tom Kiernan, who for so long had served Ireland so brilliantly as full-back and captain was not around to share in our championship triumph.

It was, however, some reward for others who had been around a long time. Ray McLaughlin, a regular in the Irish side from 1962 until 1966 before injury and domestic commitments called a temporary halt until his return in 1971; Ken Kennedy, who had come into the side in 1965 and given marvellous service as a hooker; Mike Gibson, surely one of the world's greatest players and a man who would have been great in any era. They had all come so very near to sharing in Triple Crown and championship wins, and were frustrated so many times.

I suppose the joy of winning the title, Ireland's first for twenty-three years, was in many ways less satisfactory than it would have been had we been involved in the games on that last Saturday of the championship series. Yet there was a great feeling of satisfaction and achievement nonetheless and it was some compensation for what had happened two years earlier when the programme was not completed.

There are many who are not happy with the present arrangement of playing two internationals on the same day throughout the championship. The reasons I gather for this are many, not least that it has been done at the request of big gate-taking clubs in Britain who believed that the televising of internationals was having an adverse effect on their receipts. By confining the international series to six Saturday afternoons, the problem was in part surmounted. Yet is it not possible that the new system is counter-productive? I am one who believes that television has done an immense amount for the propagation of the game.

On a more parochial theme, Ireland's win over Scotland and draw against Wales in Dublin, maintained a great sequence for Ireland at Lansdowne Road. Only once since 1967 had we been beaten, when Bob Hiller did his Cromwellian act against us in 1971 and kicked three penalty goals. It was a good record and one unequalled in the annals of Irish rugby. A few years previously we had also scored six consecutive international wins and that had not been done by an Irish side previously, nor might I add, by many sides in any era of the game.

Seven of the men who helped Ireland to win the championship were named for the Lions party to tour South Africa. Had Mike Gibson and Ray McLaughlin been available, I think it fair to argue that the quota would have been nine. I was the oldest member of the touring team, but when I accepted the invitation to lead the side, I did so secure in the knowledge that medical science was at an advanced stage in South Africa and more than one pointed out to me that if I needed a heart transplant I was going to the best possible place. I suppose it was a possibility for the very proud commander of the team they had called Dad's Army. We had lost one battle, but like good old soldiers we had won the war.

11
Triumph in South Africa

W H E N in the summer of 1973, the Four Home Unions' Committee announced that my clubmate and former international team colleague, Syd Millar, had been appointed coach to the Lions' team to tour South Africa the following summer, I thought the choice a wise one. Not everybody agreed, but that of course was their prerogative. They did not know Syd as well as I.

He had been a great prop forward for Ireland. His international career had started in 1958 and was halted in 1964. For four years, Ireland had no need of his services, something that seemed beyond my powers of reasoning, especially when injury after the Lions' tour of New Zealand in 1966, allied to business commitments, forced Ray McLoughlin out of contention for the national side. When the Irish selectors did turn again to Millar in 1968, he proved beyond reasonable doubt that his absence had been a mistake. He played well enough during the 1968 season to earn selection on the Lions tour to South Africa that summer. He had also been a member of the 1962 Lions team in South Africa and had toured in that country with Ireland in 1961. In addition he had been in the Lions team that went to New Zealand in 1959.

Against such a background of experience, Millar seemed well equipped to be able to do a really worthwhile job in South Africa, with his intimate knowledge of the country, its climatic demands and conditions and the problems generally that exist on a long tour. He had taken over as coach to the Irish team from Ronnie Dawson at the beginning of the 1972-73 season and had done a good job in that capacity. Syd is not a great theorist nor a fancy phrase-maker, but he has a tremendous knowledge of the game and I know of no shrewder tactician nor assessor of the strengths of the opposition. When Millar was appointed, it was also announced that the tour manager would be the former Welsh international, Alun Thomas. He also had a deep fund of experience as a player, was a former Lion himself having toured in South Africa in 1955. I did not know very much about him as a person, but the twin appointments seemed to be complementary.

As the 1974 season at home went on its way, there was much talk about who would lead the team. As captain of Ireland, I was obviously in the running, but at 33, I suppose there were doubts about my ability to meet the physical needs of so long and demanding a tour. As is customary, there was an immense amount of speculation in the press about the choice of captain and of course about the composition of the squad. Inevitably comparisons were made with the Lions team that had been so successful in New Zealand three years previously. Anything other than a win in the Test series would be looked on now as abject failure and that put additional pressures on all, coach, manager, captain and players.

Not the least of the factors concerning the tour was the vexed question of apartheid, a subject on which passions run high. Pressures were brought on players to refuse to play in South Africa as a mark of protest about the political regime in that country. I have no doubt at all that many who believed the Lions were wrong to go, held the most sincere and honest beliefs. I certainly respected their point of view, but I did not agree with it. I had made up my mind that if I were selected, I would go to South Africa and I also felt that the Lions presence in that country was in no way a sign of agreement with the political set-up there. I totally disagree with apartheid and its attendant evils. It is true that there are problems of race and culture in South Africa that are not taken into account by many who give strenuous opinions about them, but do so from a distance of thousands of miles, and at times some of the criticism levelled is the product of the ill-informed mind. There is however a mass of hypocrisy among some who shout about the wrongs in South Africa and who themselves condone blatant wrong nearer home. Politicians, for instance, frequently pronounce on this subject and pay lip service to the liberal line. Some of them would be better employed trying to correct the wrongs over which they themselves preside within the framework of the political institutions they help to maintain.

I believe that politics has no part to play in sport and the further politicians keep away from it, the better. Sport is used as a platform by many politicians simply because it gets great publicity and because of the intense interest in sport among the public on a general basis.

I have never believed a policy of isolation to be correct or the approach to right wrongs. Many countries have major political differences yet meet one another on the field of play in a variety of different sports. Having said that, I think it absolutely wrong that a coloured South African cannot play for his country. I think, however, that refusal by other countries to play South Africa will not in any way help the coloured population of that land of vast resources and great beauty. On the contrary, I think the Lions, by going to South Africa in 1974, brought multi-racial sport some way nearer. Nor was it my experience that the coloured population at large feel that a policy of isolation will in the long term be beneficial to them.

We played two coloured teams during the 1974 tour and I will deal with those matches further on in this chapter. It was a major breakthrough and was subsequently reflected in the composition of a multi-racial team being fielded against the French team that toured South Africa later.

Some will argue that any concession being made by the South African authorities is coming about from outside pressure. There may well be substance in that belief. Yet I cannot escape the conclusion that had the Lions not gone to South Africa in 1974, such a happening as the multi-racial team lining out in the home of South African rugby, the Newlands ground at Cape Town, would not have taken place.

Some will see the gesture by the South African authorities as merely a sop to ease the pressure on themselves. That could well be true, in which case I think that such an attitude would be a grave mistake. The South African rugby authorities are bound by the laws of the land and those laws are made by politicians, not by sportsmen. It appears certain to me, however, that a radical change in approach is needed in South Africa if they are to continue to compete internationally and to maintain the great strength of their game.

Well before the Lions went to South Africa in 1974, the British Government, or at least some members of it, had a lot to say about the tour. They were bitterly opposed to it. Frankly, I found many of the statements, especially those emanating from some quarters within the political spectrum, nothing short of a joke. Political and social injustice is not confined to South Africa. It is morally wrong however, wherever it is practised. My own country is a living proof of the evils that can exist in society, evils that too few politicians for far too long lifted a finger to rectify. The gaze was studiously averted, some obviously working on the premise that if you ignore unpleasant things they will go away of their own accord; others gave support to the maintenance of injustice.

Prior to the departure of the Lions party to South Africa early in May 1974, the British Government did not want to know us. Shortly after we arrived, instructions were sent to the British Ambassador in South Africa that no members of the embassy staff were to have anything to do with the Lions nor to attend the matches, at least officially. It was an unprecedented happening as far as I am aware. It was hard to accept the sincerity of the gesture from a government that condoned a policy laid down by its predecessors of internment without trial in my own country, Ireland.

I have no time for the destructive, whether it be perpetrated by political activists or the intolerant in pursuit of their own ends. I have no time for terrorism of word or action, nor for those who seek to cash in on success. It is not necessary to labour this point, but I was more than a little surprised when the British Government sent one of its members to London Airport to meet the Lions on their return from South Africa. Did the success of the team have any bearing on that decision, I wonder? Was it done for political expediency? Let each man be the judge, but at that I will leave the case rest.

When I was invited in March, towards the end of the International Championship, to lead the Lions to South Africa, I gladly accepted. I was excited at the prospect of going back to a country where twice previously I had been a member of a team that had lost Test series. I was looking forward to working closely with Syd Millar and was utterly convinced that we could achieve what no other country had managed this century, victory over South Africa on their own soil in a four-match Test series. There was intense debate about the composition of the squad and not everyone believed that this Lions team would return with the glory and acclaim that had surrounded the Lions in New Zealand three years previously.

Four of the players who had helped win in New Zealand declared that they were unable to undertake the trip to South Africa. They were four world class players whose loss was bound to be severe. Mike Gibson, David Duckham, Gerald Davies and Ray McLaughlin all informed the selectors that they could not travel for domestic reasons. There were suggestions that the great Welsh number eight, Mervyn Davies, would also be unavailable, but thankfully such was not the case.

Despite having to travel without some who might be considered to have been automatic selections, I still knew that we had a hard core of talent and experience in the side. I had no doubt at all for instance that we had in the squad the forwards to take on and beat the Springboks, the strength of whose game had always been based on a forward premise. Ian McLauchlan, Frank Cotton, Gordon Brown, Fergus Slattery, Mervyn Davies and Sandy Carmichael had all been in New Zealand. That was the nucleus of a great pack. The two hookers, Ken Kennedy and Bobby Windsor, were both top class. Kennedy was the more experienced of the two and had in fact been surprisingly overlooked for New Zealand, where he had toured with the Lions in 1966. Chris Ralston, prop forward, Mike Burton, flanker Tom David, Roger Uttley, Stewart McKinney, Andy Ripley and Tony Neary, were the other forwards in the squad. There was a Test pack of substance in that 16.

Among the backs, we had the best scrum-half I have ever seen, or am likely to see, in Gareth Edwards; the ideal man behind the pack and one whose experience and expertise would surely be invaluable. And so it transpired.

The backs also included John P. R. Williams, whose performances at full-back in New Zealand were nothing short of brilliant. His presence behind the three-quarter line would add substance and assurance to those in front. J. P. R. and Gareth were the only backs who survived from New Zealand, but there were others of quality in the squad. John Moloney was the second scrum-half. He had earned his place with some fine performances for Ireland. The two out-halves were England's Alan Old and Phil Bennett of Wales. Bennett had lived in the shadow of Barry John, but since John's retirement two years previously, he had emerged as a world class player in his own right. The centres were Dick Milliken and Ian McGeechan, two of the younger school of internationals; Roy Bergiers of Wales and Geoff Evans of England, two more who had their mark in the home championships, while the four wings were Tom Grace, Billy Steele, John J. Williams of Wales and Clive Rees of Wales, with Scotland's young and highly talented full-back, Andy Irvine, completing what I thought to be a good squad of players and a great collection of men. They proved to be both in a manner that went beyond the wildest dreams.

The journey to South Africa did not get the tour off to the best of starts, for a few of the players were affected by the flight, none more so than Bobby Windsor, who got a severe stomach upset and had to be taken to hospital in Johannesburg when the team arrived. Bobby is a notoriously bad traveller and is not comfortable in an airplane, however short the flight. A few of the other boys shared his anxieties.

Windsor, as befits the durable character he is, soon recovered and was back with the rest of us within two days at the team's training headquarters in Stilfontein, eighty miles from Johannesburg. He was told to watch his diet and it was during his period of convalescence that he made a remark that will live on. When he ordered an omelette, the waitress asked what kind of omelette he wanted. 'A * * * egg omelette of course, that is the only kind of omelette we have in Wales'. It was the first of many classic remarks Bobby was to make. From the outset the spirit in the squad was tremendously high. It never dropped throughout three hard months of campaigning.

There was an exceptionally big press corps with the team and I was especially pleased to see that for the first time Irish papers sent representatives. My colloborator in the writing of this book, represented *The Irish Times* while Colm Smith was there on behalf of the *Irish Independent*. There were many old friends and former travelling companions among the British Press. Vivian Jenkins of *The Sunday Times,* a former Lion himself and the veteran of the Lions' tours as a rugby correspondent. Bryn Thomas of *The Western Mail,* Terry O'Connor of the *Daily Mail,* David Frost of *The Guardian,* and Pat Marshall of the *Daily Express* had all previously toured with teams of which I was a member. There were others who like the two Irish boys were making their first Lions tour as journalists; Chris Lander of *The Daily Mirror,* and Mike Austin, of the *Coventry Telegraph,* were among these. I think they all had a happy tale to tell.

The stories the South African press had to write were not quite so happy. A visiting team can at times get it hard from the local press crew and there were attempts made to discredit the Lions on the tour. Yet there were journalists on it from South Africa that I know to be fair and knowledgeable, among them John Du Toit, Quintus Van Rooyen, Neil Cameron, and

Mike Shafto. There was, I believe, a very good relationship between players and press for the greater part, and with no television in South Africa at that time, the papers and the radio were the sources of information for the public. The BBC sent Nigel Starmer-Smith, Dewi Griffiths and Alan Williams to cover the tour for those back home, while Kim Shippey looked after the interests of the South African English-speaking population.

Perhaps nothing underlines more forcibly the degree of international interest in this tour than the huge contingent of pressmen that lived with the Lions for over three months. They soon got something to write about after our pre-tour preparations of nine days at Stilfontein, during which we became acclimatised to the altitude on the Veldt.

The first match of any tour is of critical importance and we selected a really strong side for the opening match against Western Transvaal at Potchefstroom. The performance that day was better than we expected and we won by 59 points to 13. Western Transvaal were not, it is true, reckoned to be among our most difficult opponents in the provincial games, but the standard of the Lions play that day, gave the Springboks room for considerable thought. John Moloney dislocated a shoulder in that first game and for a while it was thought he would have to go home, but skilful medical attention administered by Ken Kennedy (and what a great job he did throughout the tour to ease our pains and aches) soon had Moloney back in action.

The curtain had now gone up on the tour; the days of waiting were over, it was to be two matches a week from now until the end of July. We beat South West Africa in Windhoek in the second game of the tour and the performance was not of the vintage variety, nor might I add, was the handling of the game by the referee. Law interpretation has always caused problems on tours both by Lions teams overseas and for overseas teams visiting our shores. We had our problems in that direction in South Africa during this tour, but the major share of the controversy in this respect was reserved for the final game.

We travelled to Cape Town from Windhoek and no matter how often one goes to Cape Town, the sheer splendour of the place never fails to make an impact, especially the approach by air with the famous Table Mountain dominating the scene. However we had things other than the scenery on our mind when we arrived in Cape Town. The immediate task was against Boland at Wellington just outside the city. We had no real difficulty in winning by 33 points to 6. The next assignment was likely to be of an altogether different variety, Eastern Province at Port Elizabeth. This was a bad tempered game in which attempts were made at intimidation. Yet in retrospect the win over Eastern Province, for all the unsatis- factory aspects of the match, convinced us and I think the South Africans, that there was no way we were going to be subdued physically, and certainly we were in no mood to be scared by attempts to intimidate. Certainly there was no attempt nor concerted effort made by the Lions to seek victory by means of physical force. We had no need to resort to such methods with the talents at our disposal. The experienced members of the team were displaying their form and the younger players were blending extremely well into the scheme of things. We did however know the physical and mental de- mands that were going to be imposed on us and we were ready for them.

The fifth match of the tour put a piece of history into the record books when we beat South Western Districts by a record score of 97 points to nil. Moloney returned to the team for this game after his shoulder injury, but it was Alan Old who stole the show by scoring a try, a penalty goal and kick- ing 15 conversions with what was probably the greatest dis- play of place kicking I have ever seen.

The achievements so far on the tour were beginning to make an impact throughout the whole of South African rugby, and were of course building the morale of the players to a high pitch. Yet there was no complacency. We knew the hardest games were still ahead of us and we were especially conscious of the fact that a Test match in South Africa is something special. The 1968 Lions had a great record in the provincial games, yet lost the Test series comprehensively.

The sixth game of the tour was a close call and we were fortunate to beat Western Province at Newlands. Despite a heavy ground, the Western Province team played a quality brand of attacking rugby that day and came near to victory in a game in which the Lions did not play especially well. I believe that the performance given by Western Province had a profound influence on the thinking of the Springboks selectors when they named their team to meet us in the first Test, which was due to be played in Cape Town the following Saturday. Certainly the South African side was sprinkled with players from Western Province.. Three of the threequarters and the two half-backs were all WP men, as were flankers, Coetzee, and number eight, du Plessis. The next match for the Lions was of an historic nature, a game against the Proteas, an all coloured side, at the Goodwood stadium. There was tremendous enthusiasm in the ground and among the Proteas players, if not much technical proficiency. The match was won easily enough by the Lions, but at a high cost, an injury to Alan Old that put him out of the rest of the tour and at one time threatened to end his playing career. He received a late tackle midway through the first half and, off balance when the tackle came, his leg took the full force of it. It was a cruel blow to a player, whose form on the tour had been such that he must have had a great chance of playing in the first Test just four days later at Cape Town.

When the Lions team was selected for the Test, I think it surprised the South Africans, notably the constitution of the back row. It was decided that Fergus Slattery and Roger Uttley would play on the flanks with Mervyn Davies at number eight. Fran Cotton edged out Sandy Carmichael for the tight head berth, while Tony Neary's form on the tour had been good enough to earn a Test place, but it was felt that Slattery's type of play would best be suited to the needs.

Behind the scrum, all four threequarters were playing in a Test for the first time. J. J. Williams and Billy Steele were on the wings, Dick Milliken and Ian McGeechen in the centres, where throughout the tour and in the Test series, they did a magnificent job.

The rain fell from the heavens in plentiful supply before the First Test; we were not unhappy to see it and the playing surface was heavy. It would be a forward battle. It was, and we won it comprehensively; we also won the match by 12 points to 3, the first win by a Lions side in Cape Town in a Test match since 1938. The forwards were tremendous, and behind, Edwards was brilliant. He it was who dropped a goal that broke the heart of the Springboks challenge. They had taken the lead with a dropped goal by out-half Dawie Snyman, but after Phil Bennet equalised with a penalty, there was not much doubt about the result, for the Lions forwards were well on top and the backs played with tremendous application. The inquests in South Africa after that game were long and hard.

We returned to Newlands three days later to play Southern Universities. They fielded a useful looking side and there was always the danger of reaction following the mental and physical build up to the Test. I have never seen a worse playing surface than the one that greeted us that day in June. The pitch in parts was inches deep in water and the rain was cascading down. Incredibly, it was decided to play matches on the pitch before the Lions game against the Universities. Even without such a decision the ground was unplayable, but the referee, Dr J. Moulman, decided that the game would go on and we accepted his decision.

The Lions won easily enough, but the most fortunate thing to come out of that game was that no player on either side was seriously injured. This game was the first at which there were demonstrations against apartheid. Some students from one of the local universities invaded the pitch during the match, carrying banners. A photographer who was covering the tour, John Rubython, was removed from the field by police and the film taken from his camera. Some of the demonstrators complained of rough treatment at the hands of the police. Much of the protest apparently centred on the fact that there was objection to an all-white team being fielded by the universities with players from the multi-racial university of the Western Cape being excluded. The incidents got a fair share of publicity, but the tumult soon died down and did not distract or upset the Lions players in any way.

With Old out of the tour, the question of a replacement was now under consideration. Mike Gibson was contacted and after a few days during which he no doubt weighed all the factors concerned, particularly his domestic responsibilities, he informed Syd Millar that he would join the party, but would not be able to do so for about a fortnight.

That ruled Gibson out of consideration for the second Test which was due to take place in Pretoria, and consequently at altitude a fortnight after the Newlands game. In the meantime, there was a very close call against Transvaal in Ellis Park. Several of the Lions players were hit by an influenza virus a few days before the game against Transvaal, a game we knew would be one of the hardest of the provincial matches. But with a spirit that was absolutely typical of that which prevailed within the squad, several players lined out in the game despite feeling several degrees under. They gave of their best and revealed the character in the side by coming from behind to win by 23-15.

That match, like the one against Western Province, had a profound bearing on the thinking of the Springboks selectors, for when they announced the team for the second Test, it comprised several players from Transvaal, including the half-backs, Bayvel and ace kicker, Gerald Bosch. The Springboks were going to change their approach in an effort to win the second Test and so square the series.

The Lions in the interim set off for Rhodesia, and that provided a pleasant interlude with a visit to the Victoria Falls, the highlight of the sight-seeing expeditions. There was no difficulty for the Lions in beating Rhodesia 42-6. Four days later, came the Test in Pretoria.

Pretoria is the heart of Nationalist South Africa. It was here that one of the South Africans' most famous sons, Paul Kruger, rallied the forces during the Boer War. Perhaps the city has altered since Kruger lived in his humble surroundings there almost seventy-five years previously, but it certainly has not changed in character and outlook. The build up to the second Test was perhaps the most intense I can remember during three tours of the Republic. The whole of South Africa knew what was hanging on the match and so did we. The performance against Transvaal instilled confidence in the Springboks that they could take the Lions and so square the series. Millar steered a steady course in his preparation; once more he read the South Africans' hand perfectly. The Lions fielded an unchanged team.

It was almost impossible to move in the hotel on the morning of the match, the whole of South Africa seemed to make the Union Hotel in Pretoria their meeting place that day. The Springboks had in contrast been kept in splendid seclusion in their headquarters. They were apparently forbidden to read the papers (or so the papers said) and they trained in private.

As we set out for the ground, which was not far from the hotel, I knew in my heart we were going to win not alone that day but take the Test series.

The Lions squad had among its members some who might have earned a career as singers, pop and otherwise. One of the favourite songs was 'Flower of Scotland', with Billy Steele leading the chorus. That afternoon, we started singing it on the way to the ground. We had not completed the song when the coach pulled up outside the entrance. Not a soul in that bus moved until the song was finished. It was inspiring and indicative. When I got off the bus, I had no doubt at all that we were going to win that afternoon. We did so by a record margin.

There are those who believe that the performance given by the Lions in the second Test was one of the best they have ever seen. The boys were magnificent in all that they did. The win was perhaps the most crucial of the tour and was outstanding in method and execution. The winning margin of 19 points was the biggest recorded over a South African team in international competition. The performance answered the knockers, and there were a few despite the success the team was enjoying, who claimed that the side was playing 10-man rugby. We scored five tries that day, J. J. Williams helping himself to two, and we conceded none before 63,000 spectators in an atmosphere and in conditions that were completely different to those that obtained in the first Test.

The Springboks had made eight changes from the side that lost the first Test. Where would they now turn in an effort to halt the Lions? The win assured us that the worst we could achieve was a division of the series; we had no reason to think that we would not attain much more. Although there were many individual performances of outstanding merit that afternoon, notably by Gareth Edwards, Phil Bennett, J. J. Williams and Fergus Slattery, the win was essentially a team effort. That was how we wanted it, for above all we were a team.

Phil Bennett received a very bad ankle injury in the game that needed four stitches and it troubled him for quite a while afterwards. But Phil, a man in constant good humour (and prolific letter writer to his wife, Pat—we give him the record for most letters written and received on the tour) set off for the Kruger Park with the rest of us in good heart the following morning. The boys had earned a rest.

Mike Gibson had joined us on the day before the Test, while Alan Old, who had had an operation in a Cape Town hospital on his damaged knee, also joined the party. It was typical of Alan's bad luck that he was still not able to come to the Test match as he got a severe stomach upset on the morning of the match and spent the afternoon in bed in the hotel listening to Kim Shippey's commentary. The win had its therapeutic value for Alan however, and he soon recovered before going home, to watch a bit of cricket, as he put it.

The Kruger Park provided a pleasant interlude in the midst of our labours. Syd Millar confined the training and when we returned to Johannesburg in midweek, the team hotel had been changed. On our first visit to Johannesburg we were in a hotel that was not in any way suitable for a rugby touring team. We seemed lost in it, and requests that a change be made for our next visit, were granted and we found ourselves in the Llandrost Hotel, which proved ideal in every possible way. I would make the point here that more careful consideration should in the future be given to hotel bookings for Lions teams. While some of those we stayed in during 1974 were extremely comfortable and suitable to the needs, others were not.

The day after our return from Kruger we met the Quaggas, a team selected from the younger school of players in South Africa. The Quaggas club, of which former Scottish international Chic Henderson is a leading official, is on lines similar to the Barbarians. The side they put in the field against us was exceptionally strong—stronger than we had anticipated. Perhaps our mental attitude was not attuned for so hard a task following the second Test win and the visit to the Kruger Park. We suffered at Ellis Park that Wednesday afternoon when a record crowd of over 50,000 for a midweek game, turned out to watch us, most in the hope that we would be beaten. But we were victorious again in a controversial match during which we got two disputed tries. The referee was assaulted after the game by a spectator and there was a liberal supply of oranges and other assorted missiles thrown onto the field, not all of them at the end of the match either.

Close calls are inevitable on tours and sometimes the tourists, however strong they are, do not get away with victory. I think the win over the Quaggas once more demonstrated the dedication of heart and spirit in the Lions party. Twelve matches, twelve wins, there was talk now of going through the tour unbeaten. Most of it did not come from within the Lions party, however confident we felt in ourselves.

If there was a close call against the Quaggas, there was much more anxiety in the following game, against Orange Free State in Bloomfontein. We had a special reason for looking forward to going to Bloomfontein, the home town of our liaison officer from the South African Rugby Board, Choete

Visser, who travelled and stayed with us throughout the tour. Choete could not have done more for us. He was the ideal man for the job on hand and I have no doubt he was largely responsible for the tremendous reception we got on arrival in Bloomfontein. We were met at the airport by a cavalcade of veteran cars and driven into the town. Bobby 'The Duke' Windsor at last got the kind of treatment his status required. His 'gracious' wave to the crowd was performed with the facility of a man doing such things all his life. However Bobby was an even better hooker than he was at filling the role of royalty.

The game against the Free State was one of the hardest in which I have played. The Free State played extremely well and, with the game in injury time, were hanging on to a slender lead. Then we won a scrum against the head near their line and Gareth Edwards opened the way for J. J. Williams to get the all-important try. Without wishing to detract from the merit of the Free State performance, some of the refereeing decisions in the game were quite extraordinary, including one that led to a score for the Free State.

Kimberely is a town that many find something akin to their conception of those they see on the old cowboy films. It has its own charm of course and among its attractions is the famous 'Big Hole' from which so much of the world's wealth was extracted long ago. The diamonds are still there too, but none found their way into our possession. The rugby tradition dies hard in the area, even if in recent days the strength of the Griquas West side is not as great as it once was.

We had no difficulty in beating Griquas and one of the most satisfactory features of this match was the display of Tom Grace. He had more than his share of injury on the tour, but was now beginning to show the form that had made him an automatic selection. He scored four tries in a 69-16 win. The English winger Alan Morley also joined the party at this stage as replacement for Clive Rees who had broken a bone in a hand against the Quaggas and could take no further part in the tour. Rees had been another player for whom little went right in the way of injury. Yet despite such setbacks, and they occur in every touring party, the spirit of the players never dropped. We had tremendous character in the squad and the support I got from every player could not have been greater. I will always cherish that memory. Men such as Ian McLauchlan, Gareth Edwards, J. P. R. Williams, Mervyn Davies, all lent their experience in every possible way and made the job so much easier for the tour management.

We were into July now and had been away from home for over two months. There was still much to be done and the sixteenth match of the 22 match tour brought another very difficult game, against the South African champion province, Northern Transvaal at Pretoria. It is impossible to keep up a high level of performance in every game of so arduous a tour, and a 16-12 win over Northern Transvaal, who missed two great opportunities, led the South African press to believe as one headline put it: 'The Lions are ripe for the picking'.

We travelled on to East London to meet the coloured Bantu team, the Leopards, and any doubts that might have lingered in our minds that we had made the right decision to come to South Africa were dispelled by the reception we got from the whole population of the area outside East London in which we played. The reception was not alone warm, it was magnificent. We won the game readily enough and what was more important, Phil Bennett, who had been troubled by an ankle and knee injury since the second Test, played in the game and came through the ordeal. We needed Phil for the match four days later, the third Test at Port Elizabeth. If we were ripe for the picking then this was the time for the Springboks to bring along their baskets and gather the spoils.

Once more the Springboks made a multitude of changes— eleven to be precise—from the side that had lost at Pretoria. Once more they were influenced by what they had seen in provincial games and the side included four players from Orange Free State. The confused nature of the Springboks selectors' thought was demonstrated, however, when the day before the match they still had not decided on who would be scrum-half. That decision was taken after a practice session, which this time was not behind closed doors. They opted for Gerry Sonnekus, a recent convert to the berth from the back row. Once more it was a capacity crowd that greeted us at Boet Erasmus Stadium. The first half was furious in pace and deed. We took their initial surge which was more physically than technically proficient. The Springboks were fighting for their lives. One could understand their anxiety if not their method. We had just one change from the team that won the second Test. Andy Irvine was brought in on the right wing for Billy Steele, who had been having trouble with a rib injury. Irvine, a superb footballer and possessed of great pace, was primarily a full-back, but we believed he was adaptable enough to play on the wing, where he had been picked against Northern Transvaal the previous week. No selection ever met with better response. One of the factors that influenced his selection was his goal kicking ability and while Phil Bennett had been doing the number one job in this respect in the Tests, we had some worries about his ankle and leg injuries. Irvine kicked two penalty goals and a conversion; one of the kicks was a prodigious effort from inside our half of the field. A try just before the interval by Gordon Brown after a line-out near the Springboks, set us up for the second half, and after the interval there really was only one team in it. The pack demolished the Springboks and the backs were brilliant, especially J. J. Williams who scored two tries for the second successive occasion in the Tests. His name-sake at full-back has never played better. Phil Bennett dropped two goals and one of them will be talked about as long as the game is played. Gareth Edwards threw a reverse pass of such speed and length that Phil could have laced his boots and still had time to drop a goal. The Springboks scored three penalty goals.

So the match was won by 26 points to 9 and the series was won for we now had a winning 3-0 lead. We had not conceded a try in the series and had scored eight. Yet there still were some who said we played 10-man rugby. One of the great moments of the tour for me came at the end of the game when the whole team stood back to wave to the rest of the squad in the stand. That was our way of saying thanks for the support we had got from them. Every man had played a part in achieving an historic Test series win. Springboks invincibility on their own soil was no more. The All Blacks beaten in New Zealand, the Springboks in South Africa. Could there possibly have been greater vindication for the visionaries who a few years previously had preached the gospel of coaching and a more thorough approach?

The Springboks took their defeat well and no one was more gracious than their world-renowned president, Danie Craven. That evening at a reception in Port Elizabeth he said that he had no doubt that the Lions were the best side he had ever seen. Coming from so eminent a person, this was the zenith in compliments and it mattered very little to us that there were still the few who had little good to say about us as a team. I touched on some of the points of criticism that had been levelled at the team that evening in the Town Hall at Port Elizabeth but I have since regretted that I did so. It would have been better to leave the facts speak for themselves. However I resented attempts to undervalue what my team had done in South Africa. That night we drowned a leak, the thistle, the shamrock and the rose. Rumour has it that the following day my co-author of this book held a church parade and brought a lot of the team off to give thanks. Certainly no one could blame the South Africans for thinking that God was not on their side even if he was not an Englishman.

The mission had been accomplished, the Test series had been won. One of the points of discussion that followed in the wake of that third Test was that Mike Gibson had not been selected for the Test team. There were many factors governing his omission, but primarily the reason was that Dick Milliken and Ian McGeechan had played so well in midfield in the first and second Tests. Their defence had been splendid, their attacking ability totally complementary to the speed we had on the wings, the class at half-back and the brilliance at full-back. Mike is a world-class player, as he had proved so convincingly in New Zealand. Perhaps his greatest disadvantage was that he had joined the tour midway through. I have no doubt that the decision to stand by Milliken and McGeechan was the correct one. They had not made a mistake.

That third Test was the eighteenth match of the tour; now there were just four matches to go and an unbeaten record to preserve. Naturally thoughts were being turned towards home and it was difficult at the end of the tour for players to keep their concentration. But they did so in admirable fashion. We beat Border in East London and then defeated Natal in Durban in a match that was noted for its content of incidents than anything else. At one stage in this game, I called the players into the middle of the field to protect them from missiles thrown from the terraces. I seriously contemplated taking them off the field. The trouble had been provoked by a clash between J. P. R. Williams and Natal's flanker and captain, the distinguished international, Tommy Bedford. Things eventually quietened down and we won readily enough by 34-6.

That evening at the after-match reception Tommy Bedford had some things to say about the South African selectors that were not complimentary. But he was talking on his own ground about the game in his own country and no doubt saw the game against the Lions as a useful platform for him to air his views. As far as I was concerned, that was his prerogative.

Just before we left East London for Durban attempts were made to discredit the Lions. Stories of unprecedented revelry were printed in the South African papers, and by a few of the British papers too. I make no attempt to suggest that the Lions party was a collection of plaster saints but they were without a doubt the best behaved team I have ever travelled with. We were alleged to have had scrummage practice with naked women in the corridor of our hotel in East London. I must say I missed them if they were about; 'Mighty Mouse'

McLauchlan and the lads would have given a few tips about scrummaging, but they missed them too.

After Durban, our last port of call and our last internal air trip was to Johannesburg, where we were based for just over a week. Eastern Transvaal, at Springs on the Tuesday before the final Test, was our last provincial match. John Moloney, who had been troubled by a hamstring since we had been in Kimberely, was selected for this game even though not fully fit. Gareth Edwards badly needed a rest and Moloney willingly took the risk to give Edwards a break.

Springs was not unknown for incidents. 'Tess' O'Shea had been sent off there on the 1968 tour. Yet no one seriously thought that Eastern Transvaal would offer a serious challenge, though a few did try to argue a case for them. But we had grown used to suggestions that the next match would see our unbeaten record go by the board. The wish was father to the thought. We beat Eastern Transvaal 33 points to 10, so it was one match to go with 21 wins from 21 games. Such a circumstance could not possibly have been visualised by anyone at the outset of the tour.

We completed our preparations for the final Test at Ellis Park and were forced to make one change from the side that had clinched the series in Port Elizabeth. Gordon Brown had broken a bone in his hand and was declared unfit, so Chris Ralston was brought into the second row. We knew this was the last farewell for us and the final chance for the Springboks to salvage something from the wreckage. We were tired and thinking of the trip home two days later, yet tried to retain our concentration.

Ellis Park was packed to capacity for the game, which was refereed by Max Baise who had been in charge of the first Test, but had subsequently been omitted from the panel for the next two Tests. We played well enough in the first half and led 10-6 at the interval with Roger Uttley, who had played so very well and in some different positions on tour, getting a try that had a ring of controversy about it, some suggesting he did not ground the ball. Andy Irvine had also scored a try and Phil Bennett had converted Uttley's score. Jackie Snyman kicked two penalty goals to keep the Springboks in touch. Once more they had rung the changes, but the 75,000 crowd were behind them to a man.

In the second half, our pack showed signs of the fatigue they had so gallantly fought off during the closing period of the tour and the Springboks to their credit played better in this game than any of the other Tests. The front five held us well in the second period and we were not helped by injuries to Ian McLauchlan and Bobby Windsor, but they had their injury troubles too, Nick Bezuidenhoudt having to go off injured.

South Africa drew level after the interval when Peter Cronje scored a try that once more was controversial, there being suggestions of a knock on. But it was deemed good and that was all that mattered. Then our unbeaten record looked in peril when the Springboks took a 13-10 lead from a penalty by Snyman. The atmosphere was electric as the crowd urged the Springboks home to victory. Andy Irvine however kicked a penalty for us and we were relieved to see it going between the posts. And then just before the end came the incident which will be talked about for ever.

J. P. R. Williams came up into the line after we had won possession near the Springboks '25'. He put Fergus Slattery in possession and Slattery crashed over the line with Cronje trying to stop him from grounding the ball. I believe Slattery did score a try, but the referee ordered a five yards' scrum. We won possession and J. J. Williams made a dash for the line but was held short and the referee blew the full time whistle. We had failed to land a 100 per cent record, but we remained unbeaten.

The draw in some ways was very disappointing. Yet we might have lost and I feel that despite the try-that-never-was, a draw was probably a fair result to the game. The South Africans were certainly happy to get it at any rate, for they chaired their captain Hannes Marais from the field.

Like us on previous tours, it was now the Springboks' turn to absorb the lessons handed out during the tour. We said our farewells at the reception that evening. I knew that I had played my last match for the Lions. It had been my pleasure to travel with them five times. I had never shared the company of a better bunch of fellows than those who played with me in South Africa in 1974.

There are only two aspects of that tour that bring unhappy memories to me now. Two of those who were in our party have died. Pat Marshall died suddenly in the summer of 1975. He had been a great tourist and a good friend of mine over many years. He was also a great lover of rugby football.

The second person was a man for whom I had the deepest affection. Dr Jamesy Maher was medical officer to the Irish team, following my father-in-law, the late Harry Michael into that post. Jamesy had gone to South Africa as a supporter and joined us midway through the tour. There was no more genial or decent man in every aspect of his being than Jamesy. He was a friend not alone to every Irish player, but to every rugby player. A man with a unique capacity for doing good; a Christian gentleman in every respect. Jamesy died shortly before Christmas 1975. His funeral was a demonstration of the esteem in which he was held. I am proud to have known him and prouder still to be in a position to have called him my friend and know that it was true in every respect.

12
Evolution and Revolution

It was my fortune to play in international rugby for a period of fourteen years from 1962 until 1975. Sixty-three games for Ireland, five Lions' tours and seventeen Test appearances are far in excess of anything a man has a right to expect. Indeed one international cap is more than the great majority of players are lucky enough to attain. Irrespective of how many a player does get, one has no moral right to expect or take for granted selection for his country.

The period in which I played at representative level was arguably the most revolutionary in the game's history. Since rugby became an organised game in its own right and put into international competition over a century ago, there have been many changes. Tactics evolved, some in the last century that still hold good to this day, its own commentary on the profound thinkers within the game from the outset in the Victorian era.

The first international between England and Scotland in 1871 was played with 20 players to each team. Thus the first major alteration in the structure and approach of the game could be said to have been the reduction in the playing numbers to 15 a-side. That change came in the later seventies and Ireland played in the initial international involving the 15 a-side game. So it could be said that Ireland played a major role in the first really important change tactically and technically. Throughout every era, men's minds have been turned towards perfecting the skills and tactics within the game. Yet I think it is true to say that change was basically slow and an ultra-conservative approach and indeed at time blatant resis-

I

tance to change was the order. Without arguing the case further I think there is ample evidence to support the validity of that claim.

Wales, with their facility for the running game, not surprisingly led the way in standardising threequarter play by playing four men in the line. The great All Blacks side of 1906 brought their own brand of variety to the game by the use of their captain Gallacher to put the ball into the scrum even though he was a forward. History recalls that such a tactic was frowned on by the powers in the game at the time. The use of the wing forward in a specific role detached from the multiple duties that the forwards of old were asked to perform, came early in the century with Ireland's Charles Vaughan Rooke among the very early exponents of this ploy. The role of the wing forward was a bone of contention for the better part of 50 years and indeed it is not so long ago that the laws were altered to curb his activities and to give more room to the opposing half-backs.

The laws of the game are the responsibility of the International Board, a body conceived in the 1880's on an Irish initiative after a dispute between Scotland and England on a point of law. I think the Board has served the game very well, even if in the near future the spread of the game to the American continent and to the further reaches of Europe may necessitate a broader vision in relation to its make-up, which is now the exclusive preserve of what are known as the major rugby playing nations, the four home countries, South Africa, New Zealand and Australia. The omission of France for instance seems to me something of a contradiction, for here is a major rugby playing nation that in the post-war era has proved a match for all-comers. The French like to maintain an independent line, thus allowing themselves more freedom. I fully accept that one would have to look very carefully at the game in the emerging nations, its construction and approach. Yet for long soccer in these islands was strong enough to hold a firm line and basically go its own way independent of the controlling body F.U.F.A. Indeed in the early years of the

World Cup, the home countries did not think it worth while to participate. Things have undergone radical change in the last 40 years; now the World Cup is the most prized of all trophies in the soccer world.

The time may not be too far distant when events could catch up with the International Board if the game of rugby continues to spread at a rapid rate. Doubtless the authorities are keeping in close touch with all developments in the countries not now under their control. I headed this chapter 'evolution and revolution' advisedly. I know that I have played in a period of maximum development in the game. The change in attitude for instance that has taken place in so many spheres of rugby during my playing career has been astonishing over a period of 15 years.

When I first came into the Irish side in 1962, preparation for an international was not so much limited as almost non-existent. I am not implying that there was not total commitment to victory or that great thinkers and tacticians were lacking. It was however a question of attitude and scope. The only coaches we knew about were the kind that took us to and from the grounds. The captain was in charge of pre-match training and that was confined to a run out on the day before the match. I think it true to say that top players in all eras devoted a lot of attention to physical fitness, but more often than not they were groping in the dark. National selectors had a major say in team preparation, that is those of them who sought involvement. In my experience, the advice often offered in the early part of my representative career was all too often a medley of confusion. Yet I was fortunate to play under a man of the calibre of Bill Mulcahy, a great player, a fine captain and a good friend. I feel certain that had Mulcahy been the product of a later period, his impact would have been even greater than it was. His problems were that he was the prisoner of the system he inherited. Had I been in his position at that time, I have no doubt things would have been the very same.

One incident in the early part of my career keeps coming

back to me at times. I reflect in retrospect on whether or not things were quite as haphazard as they seem to have been. I can well remember shortly after I played in my first international, talking to a selector who kept calling me Mick. For a while I could not understand this, it could scarcely be put down to some Englishmen's facility for referring to all Irishmen as 'Micks'. The selector concerned was Irish and had helped pick the Irish team. I found out later that when he was talking to me, he thought he was in fact in conversation with Mick Hipwell. I do not think I bear any resemblance to Mick Hipwell, for one thing he is better-looking than me, or so he would probably tell me; for another, Mick was a back row forward. Even now when I think about that, I often wonder if I owe my selection, or at least one selector's vote, to the quality of Mick Hipwell's play or whether Mick owes his selection to mine. As Mick was out of the Irish team for a long period from 1962 to 1968, he may well attribute the gap to the case of mistaken identity. That incident is rather typical of the approach of some to the duties of selection in my early days, but it certainly is not characteristic of all; yet I could not possibly visualise such a happening today.

The first great change came with the advent of Ray McLoughlin as captain of Ireland in 1965. I have briefly touched earlier on his capacity for leadership; I now deal with it in greater detail.

He had come into the Irish team on the same day as I made my debut against England in 1962. It was obvious to me from my first encounter with him that here was a man of high intelligence and with profound depth of thought. Allied to these attributes was a great physical strength and skill as a prop forward who could play with equal facility on either side of the scrum.

McLoughlin is a meticulous man; his is an ordered mind and anything other than a thorough and dedicated approach to any task he undertook would not be compatible with his character. He saw that change was needed in approach and he acted. In doing so, there is no doubt at all that he upset the *status quo* and eclipsed the powers of some on the administrative side of the game. He believed in total involvement, and what is more important, total commitment to the task he was given. He could be said to have been a revolutionary, and I say now without hesitation that the game, not alone in Ireland, but in general terms owes a debt to Ray McLoughlin that will never be repaid. His contribution was inestimable, yet like many another visionary, he paid the price of rejection at a time when he had so much more to give as a captain and a leader.

Under McLoughlin's leadership, the whole approach to preparation for internationals changed. He tolerated no interference with his conception of what was necessary before an international. He analysed the opposition. He sought and got greater application to training and he brought to it a method that unfortunately did not come to full fruition under his guidance. From the outset, he had his critics and they were not all administrators. There were players who found the task of total commitment, beyond their mental and physical capacities. I do not argue a case that all McLoughlin's theories were correct, but I am absolutely sure that the basic premise of his methods and approach were right. I would go further and say that time and events have proved him to have been correct in what matters most, the basic philosophy applicable to international rugby.

It is often stated that a good captain is a winning captain. McLoughlin was both. Some believe that he was too inflexible and at times sacrificed some things to the theory of tactics not altogether suited to some of the players he had at his disposal. I do not subscribe to that belief. He took over leadership of the Irish side at a time when we were beaten more often than not. Recourse to the statistics will prove the point. For instance from the time I came into the Irish side in 1962 until McLoughlin took over as captain in 1965, we won two matches. McLoughlin believed that a change in mental attitude and approach would bring its own benefits, especially as Ireland now had emerging several players who had the obvious potential to be great. I have in mind such as Mike Gibson, Ronnie Lamont, Ken Kennedy, Roger Young, all of whom won their first caps in 1965. There was a hard core of experience on hand too with Tom Kiernan, Jerry Walsh, Kevin Flynn, Bill Mulcahy and Noel Murphy, all men of proven ability.

McLoughlin quickly brought results. In 1964, we won one match, against England at Twickenham. That season, we ended with the wooden spoon. We drew with France in the first game of McLoughlin's captaincy and then went on to beat England and Scotland. We went to Cardiff to play Wales and the game was a Triple Crown match for both teams. McLoughlin was the new Messiah to the Irish rugby public. However, that fickle force that loves a winner and does not want to know a loser, got food for criticism when Wales beat us in Cardiff.

It mattered little that we lost to a fine Welsh side or that we missed chances in the early stages, notably from penalty opportunities on a day when the Arms Park ground was saturated from persistent heavy rain before and during the match, in which another great Irish back, David Hewitt, returned to the side. The atmosphere that day in Cardiff was electric and the going was hard, so hard in fact that the referee spoke to both captains during the first half and asked them to cool down their players. Wales scored a try just before half time and Terry Price converted with a great kick. From then on, Wales were the better side and thoroughly deserved to win.

The murmurs about Ray McLoughlin's captaincy that had been subdued by his rapid rate of success now grew louder, as they invariably do from the lips of those who seek safety in numbers and fabric for their dissent in failure, irrespective of whether or not the failure is caused by the man whom they seek to discredit. I was subsequently to learn similar lessons to those McLoughlin had to endure from the ranks of the prejudiced.

So McLoughlin had failed to deliver the Triple Crown, he had not failed in his primary task of captaincy. That season

South Africa came on a short tour of Ireland and Scotland in April and McLoughlin had the privilege of leading Ireland to victory over the Springboks, Ireland's first win over South Africa.

The following season, he was again appointed captain and was warm favourite to lead the Lions to Australia and New Zealand in the summer of 1966. As events transpired he was not to end that season as Ireland's captain. We lost to France, in Paris, drew with England at Twickenham, lost to Scotland at Lansdowne Road and for the game against Wales in Dublin, McLoughlin was relieved of his task of leadership, which was taken over by Tom Kiernan. McLoughlin never again captained an Irish side, but he altered things beyond recall. That is his monument.

Major changes in approach were at hand throughout the whole structure of the game in the home countries. Suddenly there was talk about coaching, method, preparation. There was, inevitably a resistance from those who did not want things to change. There were cries about amateurism, and the ethos of the game in general. In the meantime, the All Blacks and Springboks went on winning the test series against the Lions. What happened in the Southern Hemisphere did not seem to bother the conservatives within the framework of rugby football on the home front. Not even after the Lions returned from New Zealand after an inglorious Test series in 1966, did some get the message. New Zealand came to Britain in 1967 and showed the true value of coaching, method and the full use of great resources. That tour, which did not incorporate Ireland because of an outbreak of foot and mouth disease in Britain, opened the eyes of a few and quickly confirmed the more progressive element in their belief that radical change was needed. The Lions went to South Africa in 1968 and again lost the Test series. Yet that series was, in many ways, the springboard for the first major push towards a more thorough and methodical approach on the British and Irish scene. Ronnie Dawson, the Lions' coach in South Africa and a man who had seen what was required to be done, hammered the message home when he returned from South Africa. He spelled it out in terms that were loud and clear. We either adopted different methods or else contented ourselves with being perennial losers against the All Blacks and Springboks.

Dawson, captain of Ireland just before my advent to the national team, had been in the Ray McLoughlin mould as a captain, but was the victim of circumstances and events during his term of leadership. The minds of those who mattered were not yet attuned to the need for change. McLoughlin was fortunate that he came later, if only a little.

Wales was the first of the home countries to appoint a coach to their national team, former international David Nash being entrusted with the task. The demands in Ireland for a similar line of action began to gather impetus and finally, in 1970, Ronnie Dawson was appointed. England and Scotland, too, did likewise and the whole face of the game was rapidly altered. The provinces in Ireland, with Ulster and Leinster first in the field, decided to appoint coaches to their teams. Dawson had filled the role for Leinster before taking over at national level and Ken Armstrong, another dedicated to the progress and evolution of the game, was in charge of the Ulster side. At club level the structure came under close examination and the attitude was reflected throughout the game. Now great events were at hand. There were still some who held firm to their resistance, but the first crack in their defence came when the South Africans visited Britain and Ireland in 1970 and caught the first winds of the new climate that prevailed in the home of the game. There were few easy games for touring teams now. The regional and provincial sides that a few years previously would put up the gallant fight before going down to defeat at the hands of the All Blacks and Springboks, were now a tougher proposition. Preparation was reflected in results on that tour. It was suggested that the anti-apartheid demonstrations that took place were the main cause of the Springboks' problems; I do not subscribe to that view, however upsetting some of the demonstrations may have been to the tourists' concentration.

The big test was at hand however in the Lions' tour to New Zealand in the summer of 1971. The results and the outcome of the Test series on that tour broke the last vestige of anything remotely approaching sensible argument about the wisdom of the gospel of coaching. Carwyn James had carried on magnificently where Ronnie Dawson had left off in South Africa three years previously. There could not have been a better choice than James to mould the resources at his disposal.

There is nothing like victory to prove a point and the Lions' Test series win in New Zealand proved beyond all reasonable doubt that the revolution in the game in Britain and Ireland had brought benefits not alone more rapidly than one might reasonably have expected, but gave the game of rugby a new dimension in the part of the world where it had originated, yet had been allowed to stagnate for far too long. Ray McLoughlin was in New Zealand to share in the triumph; he could afford to smile, graciously of course, as is his wont.

The young players who came into the clubs from the schools at this period came into club rugby at a time when just about every committee in the land were taking a new look at their facilities. Adequate training facilities were now a top priority. No longer was training a quick few laps of the field and a shower. Thoughts were turned towards the provision of gymnasia, adequate lighting around the grounds for training purposes, greater attention to the prevention and treatment of injuries. These were the tangents that flowed from the great re-think of the late sixties. Not alone is rugby a better game because of it, both to play and to watch, it has also brought many attendant assets to clubs quite outside the playing realms. There is for instance much greater family involvement, my own club Ballymena being a typical example. Now wives, who once stayed at home, come along with the children and enjoy the facilities of the clubhouse, the children get a feeling for the game and its atmosphere from a very young age. Greater physical fitness and technical proficiency has also, to a large extent, eradicated much rough and foul play from the game, contrary to the suggestions that rugby is getting more physical and losing its character. There has been much publicity in recent times about players being sent off and suggestions that rugby is getting progressivly dirtier. I do not agree with such views.

The game, in essence, is such that there is room in it for those with malice in their minds to indulge in foul deeds. There is opportunity for the mischief-makers and I do not suggest that the game is free of them. It is my experience that they do not survive for long.

Rugby has its different characteristics in every nation. The crowds at Twickenham, for instance, are totally different to those at the Arms Park and Lansdowne Road, where passion and enthusiasm flow more freely from the spectators. The atmosphere at Murrayfield is perhaps the most staid of all grounds on which I have played at international level. In South Africa, one finds the desire to win almost fanatical and defeat is akin to a national disaster. The New Zealanders are passionate and knowledgeable. Yet there is a common denominator among rugby crowds the world over, and that is a great love for the game. It is reflected in different ways, yet one seldom finds spectators who go to matches to indulge in activities that give reign to their baser instincts or to indulge in mob warfare on the terraces. It has remained markedly free from such happenings; hopefully such will always be the case. On a more narrow aspect, the alterations in approach to international matches gradually brought with it a more liberal attitude to the players involved in the big games.

I felt for a long time, however, that a parsimonious attitude was prevalent among officials in relation to the Irish side. There were petty rules and regulations that were at least an irritation and at best an inconvenience; restriction on menu, for instance, and too many things one was not supposed to do. I am fully aware that Rugby Union is an amateur game and that great pains are taken to keep it strictly amateur. I fully endorse any protection that the administrators take to keep it so. Yet it is a fact (and in the present climate of economic recession and scarcity of money, I think the problems are over-emphasised) that playing rugby is not alone time-consuming but is also a costly exercise. When I got my first pair of football boots, they cost thirty shillings. Today, such a sum would hardly buy a good pair of football stockings. Such things as stockings and jerseys are, of course, supplied for international matches, but the traditional custom of jersey swapping can prove a costly exercise. Just before last season for instance Irish players were informed that they could retain only two jerseys in any one season. A sum of £10 would have to be paid by the player for every other jersey retained. That is a prohibitive sum, especially for the married players and those who are students. It imposed an unfair burden on players many of whom might not want to exchange a jersey with an opponent from a country whose jersey he already had among his souvenirs. But it is extremely difficult to say no.

What about relations with the Press? It is natural that players on the international scene, and at home in the inter-provincial series, come into more contact with the Press than the ordinary club player. I have many good personal friends among journalists, yet it is true to say that at times I have felt some of their criticism after tour games and internationals was too severe, and not always based on fact. However, maybe I was too near the scene and the players involved to be totally objective.

Both in Ireland and in Britain and much further afield, I have had a lot of contact with the news media; this was especially true when I led the Lions and Ireland. Inevitably, my contact with the Irish and British Press was greater than in any other country, and while I have often disagreed with journalists' assessments, I have found them personally to be decent men in every sense of the word. They have, after all, a job to do. Criticism is the name of the game, and the higher you go the more vulnerable you are. My greatest objection through the years has been to the journalist who has gone beyond the bounds of reasonable comment and allowed prejudice not only to colour his judgement, but to pervert the truth.

The Press—indeed all the media—have a vital role to play in the development and propagation of rugby.

13
The Great Ones

INTERNATIONAL team selections, irrespective of the
country, always arouse tremendous interest, even among people
who do not patronise matches, international or otherwise. I
have met people who held strong views of the constitution of
Irish teams that I knew never went near a rugby match.

I suppose, in part, their opinions were coloured by what they
read in the papers or what they had seen on television which
has brought rugby into the homes of many who knew nothing
and cared less about the game. The vast coverage of the big
games on television has brought with it, I believe, a new breed
of rugby followers, even if their watching is confined to an
armchair in front of the fire on cold winter Saturday afternoons.

There are few more contentious issues than national sides,
therefore it is with trepidation that I play the game so beloved
of rugby journalists, picking an international team. My team,
however, will know no international frontiers; it is a selection
of those whom I believe to be the best players I have played
with and against over a period of 15 years.

The more I dwell on the task, the more awesome it appears.
When I put forward the theory that the period of my involvement in representative rugby brought with it some of the
greatest players the game has known, I would not wish such a
suggestion to be taken by anyone as a personally selfish
acclamation. Far from it. Yet if one studies rugby history, and
I think when our successors come to study the period in the
game that extended through the sixties and seventies, it will
stand out as an era of great significance. In another chapter,

I deal with the evolution that took place, but I think it pertinent to make the point as a preface to the side that I am going to name.

The wider and more rounded the experience, then the broader the horizons must be for the selector, amateur or otherwise. Having played in 80 internationals for Ireland and the Lions, it is inevitable that I encountered all the great ones from the major rugby playing nations. I think I could probably pick five or six teams that would all give each other a really hard game. Yet such an exercise would be to surrender the challenge posed in the make-up of the 'greatest' side.

The tactical changes that have taken place over the past decade have been quite astonishing and of course must weigh with me in selecting a team. Therefore it might be argued against my selection that, in some respects the basic premise is therefore unfair, the advantage being with the modern players. I accept such a proposition, yet seek my answer in the inevitability of time. Players may have been great in one era who would not have reached similar status or acclaim in another.

I am immediately confronted with the problem when I start by naming the best full-back of my time. The man I played with most often at the top level was my old friend and Ireland and Lions colleague for a decade, Tom Kiernan. Kiernan was perhaps the best positional player I have seen in the full-back berth. His anticipation was uncanny, his hands as safe as the Bank of England, his line kicking long and accurate. He was quick too and had a very sharp football intellect. Yet he was the product of a type of full-back play that was superseded near the end of his career. Today's full-back is required to act very often in the role of a fifth threequarter. Kiernan got a lot of criticism for not coming up into the line often enough when his reign was coming to an end in the early seventies. Much of the criticism was unfair, for it was seldom pointed out that he indeed had a spirit of adventure in this respect when it was not considered prudent for full-backs to make advances forward in the interests of safety. The younger breed of players came forward more than Kiernan, and some were possessed of greater flair. Had Kiernan emerged 10 years later than he did, I feel sure he would have been a great attacking full-back. As it is, I have not seen better in terms of the basics of full-back play.

However I cannot find a place in my team for Kiernan, because the full-back berth in my line-up must go to John P. R. Williams of Wales. I use the term magnificent in relation to Williams and I use it advisedly. There are times when Williams probably makes mistakes in defensive situations; I have in mind particularly a game against Ireland at Lansdowne Road in 1970. Yet such errors are very rare and I think entirely due to his burning competitive spirit and his anxiety to attack even from near his own line. He is a prolific scorer of tries, the best helper a threequarter ever had. A tackler of devastating effectiveness and courage that is total. Williams thrives on competition and would have been great in any position he had chosen to make his own. He has been full-back for Wales since 1969 and has made a major contribution to their many successes since then. He was full-back for the Lions in New Zealand in 1971 and for the Lions in South Africa in 1974. Without him, I very much doubt if the Lions would have enjoyed the degree of success they did on those two tours. I do not think he dropped even one ball in South Africa and that is its own testimony to his ability in a country that is so demanding and where more often than not the ball comes out of a very bright sky. His performances have been unsurpassed in my experience.

I will follow the orthodox line and go next to the right wing; and if some will ask what does an ignorant forward know about back play, then I must say that I call it as I see it and I have not seen a better wing than Gerald Davies, of Wales. To see Davies in full flight is to see art in motion. He is very quick, a beautifully balanced runner, good in defence; in general terms the wing who has most impressed me. On the left, I think I would go for a winger different in character and approach to Davies, the New Zealander, Grant Batty.

Batty is of a sturdier build than Davies and not as graceful to watch. Yet he is a prolific scorer, a hard competitor and a good footballer. His closest rival would be J. J. Williams of Wales, a real speed merchant who has emerged on the international scene in the past four years and who contributed so much to the Lions' success in South Africa in 1974. But Batty is the more durable of the pair, and probably better in defence.

In many ways the easiest positions I have found to fill, are in that most vital of midfield areas, the centre. Without hesitation, I would go for a combination of Mike Gibson of Ireland, and John Dawes of Wales. Gibson is the most capped back in the world and whether or not he was born an Irishman, I do not think it would have made any difference for he would still be the most capped back in the world in any country, however deep the reservoir of talent. He is a superb footballer, a brilliant reader of the game, outstanding in the essential basics of passing and handling and if he has a fault it is his inclination to lay off the tackle in an attempt to avert imminent danger elsewhere. This has earned him some criticism. He made the move from out-half, where he played in international rugby from 1964 to 1969. He was a world class out-half; he is a world class centre.

Some may be surprised that I have gone for John Dawes as Gibson's partner. There were probably centres who did some things better than Dawes, but he was another great reader of the game, a really solid player in the midfield, a great passer of the ball and I think totally complementary to Gibson. They proved their effectiveness as a pair during the tour to New Zealand in 1971. I would also ask Dawes to captain my side. I have not played with or against a better leader of a team or of men. His contribution to Wales in this capacity has been invaluable, and to the Lions whom he led so skilfully in New Zealand.

When selecting the half-backs, once more I think in terms of a pair, and I honestly do not have undue difficulty in once more going for a Welsh combination, that of Gareth Edwards and Barry John. I have seen and played with and against some great scrum-halves, but none to compare or even seriously challenge Edwards, one of the most complete footballers I have seen.

Edwards is a master of every facet of scrum-half play. I have come to appreciate his qualities as team-mate and opponent. His passing from either side is of phenomenal length; his line kicking, inch accurate and exceptionally long. His speed of thought and movement and reading of situations in defence and attack put him in a class apart. He is not a big man in stature by any means, but then scrum-halves are not usually big; yet he is very well built and capable of taking an extreme amount of punishment. He has often been the target for those who want to take him out of the game by any means, but his reflexes are quick and his agility and intellect so alert, his elimination is a task that has proved beyond the reach of most.

It was Barry John's extreme good fortune to play his international rugby with Edwards and I have no doubt that such an asset went a long way towards building up the reputation of 'The King', as John was christened on his return from the Lions' tour of New Zealand in 1971. Nevertheless John was an out-half of great skill and speed. He was a splendid kicker of the ball, yet had had equal facility for setting up his backs for the menacing movements. A really complete footballer, I do not find it difficult to believe that John was also a soccer player of exceptional merit.

I do not want to leave the half-back positions without reference to some other greats that unfortunately disposition of time and other factors do not permit me to accommodate in my team. Anyone would be happy to have such scrum-halves in their side as Dawie de Villiers of South Africa, Sid Going and Chris Laidlaw of New Zealand, Ken Catchpole and John Hipwell of Australia. Then other great backs in my time were such wings as Christian Darrouy of France, David Duckham of England, my Irish team-mate Tom Grace, now at the top of his international career. Alan Duggan, a prolific try scorer for Ireland, Arthur Smith of Scotland, the first man under whom I played for the Lions on tour in South Africa in 1962.

145

K

At out-half, one thinks of wonderful players like Phil Bennett of Wales, Gordon Waddell of Scotland, Phil Hawthorne of Australia, Mac Herwini and Earl Kirton of New Zealand, Peter Visagie of South Africa and Pierre Albaladejo of France.

The more one parades the names of players such as these, the more doubtful one becomes about the wisdom of the selection on which I have finally settled. And the list of names I have produced by no means exhausts the panel of magnificent backs of my time.

I suppose that as a forward, I must treat the construction of my pack as something really special. Yet it may surprise many that I had less difficulty in settling on my final combination up front than I had behind the scrum. Perhaps I view forward play with a more dedicated eye, despite the fact that so many believe that education and playing as a rugby forward are quite incompatible. Don't believe it! This is propaganda to which the rugby public are constantly subjected by the 'league of backs'.

Whatever about the dedicated eye and the perceptive mind, I speak with some first-hand knowledge about the eight men I would ask to form my forward division. Having formed it, I am not altogether sure either, that I would relish the prospect of playing them, at least not at my present age. Perhaps the initial surprise in the selection is that it would be a three-country outfit. That has nothing whatever to do with team work, although I believe the eight I have chosen would blend into a magnificent unit. I would hand the leadership of the forwards to Ray McLoughlin. He and that great All Black Ken Gray, I would have at prop. That means no room for some who were my colleagues in scores of Homeric battles all over the world and I have particular regret at having to leave out Ian McLauchlan of Scotland, whose exploits on the Lions tour to New Zealand in 1971 earned him the appellation of 'Mighty Mouse'. I could argue a case for many others, but in my heart I could not sustain an argument against Ray McLoughlin and Ken Gray.

My period in international rugby strangely coincided with

146

a time when almost every country in the game produced a hooker to eclipse the feats of others who had occupied the position previously. Foremost in this respect one thinks of Ireland's Ken Kennedy, the world record holder for caps as a hooker. Then there is John Pullin of England, Richard Benisis of France, G. F. Malan of South Africa, Frank Laidlaw of Scotland, Peter Johnson of Australia, and the man for whom I opt, Bryn Meredith of Wales. Meredith was near the end of his international career when I was starting mine, but in general terms and for all round effectiveness, he was the best I have yet seen.

I think I can claim intimate knowledge of the second row, or as the moderns prefer to refer to it as lock, a term once bestowed on the man packed down in the middle of the back row, now referred to as number eight. Just about everyone will be expecting me to opt instantly for my old adversary and friend, Colin Meads of New Zealand. They are correct. The man they call 'Pine Tree' in New Zealand has been aptly named, there can have been few if any better than him in the history of the game. It has often been said of him that he was too physical and unnecessarily so. Perhaps there is some truth in it, yet he was magnificent for all that, and a more profound thinker on the game than some have suggested. He was great in the line-out, and astute with it. He was a good psychologist too, incredibly strong in ruck and maul and very quick for a big man. Who goes in with Meads? That was much more difficult than naming the big fellow.

Frik Du Preez of South Africa is certainly a front runner, so too was Johan Classen of South Africa, whom I encountered early in my career and whose ability helped appreciably in my education of second row play. Coming forward a little there is Gordon Brown of Scotland, and going back Billy Mulcahy, the man who captained the first Irish side I played on. The list is long for any that I encountered in international rugby gave me a fair share of trouble. But after weighing all the issues and assessing all the attributes, I go for Colin Meads's brother, Stan.

147

Here was a second row forward of real substance. He is overshadowed in that vague force, the public mind, by Colin's deeds, but Stan Meads was a great player in his own right and would have been great in any era. He was a good ball winner and good ball carrier, and I think the ideal partner for 'Pine Tree'.

Now my task is nearly done, but not quite for I still have to construct that very important area, the back row, the fountain from which flows so much that is vital. Once more I make the suggestion that in the period of maximum development of the game that my career embraced, the back row men played a major part in the evolution and tactical alterations. I have particularly in mind the All Blacks, who needless to add are represented in my outfit. In fact, two of the three for whom I have settled are New Zealanders, Ian Kirkpatrick and Wacka Nathan. I would have them on the flanks and between them, that prince of number eights, Mervyn Davies of Wales.

That unit embraces all that is best in back row play. Hard and physical, yet delicate in appreciation of the requirements. Strong and resolute in defence, devastating in attack. Ball players and ball winners, a trio that represents height and strength without any sacrifice to mobility.

So yet again there is no room for a great collection of players who would be in many another side of greats picked by minds probably more astute than mine. I leave on the sidelines many whom I would be proud to have in any team I played on. Budge Rogers of England, Fergus Slattery of Ireland, Jan Ellis of South Africa, Noel Murphy of Ireland, Jim Telfer of Scotland, Michael Crauste of France, Kel Tremain of New Zealand, Dai Morris of Wales, among the flankers. No room for Benoit Dauga of France, a great at number eight or second row. Ken Goodall of Ireland, whose international career was all too short because he turned professional. Brian Lochore, who led so brilliantly the 1967 All Blacks on their tour of Britain, or Doug Hopwood of South Africa.

So here is the team I have decided upon. I put it forward

without the slightest doubt that it will probably cause more controversy among rugby men than any selection produced by a national selection committee. J. P. R. Williams (Wales); G. Davies (Wales), M. Gibson (Ireland), J. Dawes (Wales), capt., G. Batty (New Zealand); B. John (Wales), G. Edwards (Wales), R. J. McLoughlin (Ireland), B. Meredith (Wales), K. Gray (New Zealand), C. Meads (New Zealand), S. Meads (New Zealand), W. Nathan (New Zealand), M. Davies (Wales), I. Kirkpatrick (New Zealand).

It is a side well loaded with players from New Zealand and Wales. That certainly owes something to the fact that both countries produced great sides in my particular time. I think their records will sustain that opinion. No players from England, Scotland, Australia, France, or South Africa; maybe that is a measure of the awesome strength of the 15 players I have chosen; maybe it is a reflection on my judgement. But I would stand by that team to beat any selection put into the field against it. Missing are some whose names will be forever enshrined in the game, not just within their own particular political boundaries, but throughout the world of rugby. I have regrets at the omission of so many, but I make no apologies.

14
Back to Base

WHEN I returned from South Africa in July 1974, I had absolutely no intention of retiring. I felt as fit as at any time in my career and in any case, the 1974-75 season was the centenary year of the I.R.F.U. How could the front line of Dad's Army such as Ray McLoughlin, Ken Kennedy, McBride and Sean Lynch contemplate such a drastic measure as retirement, even if some thought we had been around just about as long as the Union itself?

It is customary on return from a Lions' tour to take a rest and not resume playing until about the beginning of December. This was an exceptional year, however, for Ireland was due to meet the President's XV in Dublin on 6 September. This President's XV was, in essence, a world team with players from all the major rugby playing nations with the exception of New Zealand, who were due to come to Ireland in November and play six games as part of the centenary celebrations.

The geriatric unit was still intact when the team to meet the President's XV was announced. It was, too, a fairly formidable visiting team and it was for Ireland a full international as caps were awarded. The team that had played in Ireland's last championship game the previous season was intact and we drew 18 points all on a miserably wet afternoon at Lansdowne Road. It certainly was not the kind of weather that lent itself to celebration, yet the game was quite good and it was an achievement to draw with an opposing force that included Gareth Edwards, Phil Bennett, J. J. Williams, Bobby Windsor, Ian McLauchlan, Tony Neary, Alan Esteve of France, Andy

Irvine, Andy Ripley, Ian McCallum of South Africa, and Garrick Fay of Australia.

Those who had played on the Lions' tour took a rest after the President's match, but the next assignments for us all were games against the All Blacks. They came to celebrate the centenary of the I.R.F.U., but we had no doubt at all they were also coming to re-establish themselves in the wake of the 1971 defeat by the Lions and the disappointments of the 1972-73 tour in Britain and Ireland.

I believe the results they got indicate very clearly that they achieved their objective. They won all their games in Ireland, beat a Welsh XV in Cardiff and then drew with the Barbarians at Twickenham. One of the most noticeable of their improvements was in their scrummaging and none of the sides that met them were able to establish any clear-cut superiority in this respect. Their line-out play and technique were excellent and their support play, as always, was first class. They were led by Andy Leslie, a comparatively unknown player, but a number eight of great class and a splendid captain. They had Sid Going at scrum-half and he dictated the pattern of play behind the scrum. Although they had Grant Batty and Bryan Williams on the wings, they were not especially fluent behind the scrum, but they were very thorough and made few errors. The All Blacks were back and in many ways that was to be expected. They are quick learners and soon eradicated the deficiencies that the Lions had exposed in their play and those that had been evident on the 1972-73 tour.

They left for home before Christmas and did so having beaten Ireland 15-6 at Lansdowne Road. There was no doubt they thoroughly deserved the win as their forwards out-played us. Two of the Irish pack playing in that game were not to play for Ireland again, prop Sean Lynch and number eight Terry Moore. They had given great service to Ireland.

The end of the year brought to me personally unexpected honours on a scale that would not have been possible only twelve months previously. Rugby authorities had frowned on such awards as 'Rugby Player of the Year' but they had

151

relented after much criticism in 1973 when Mike Gibson was named as winner of the Texaco Award as Ireland's player of the year. Yet he was forbidden to take the trophy. It was a strange decision when one considered the fact that the various rugby unions were at that time accepting sponsorship, even if on a limited scale. Advertisements surrounded Lansdowne Road and other grounds. It thus seemed a rather inconsistent decision to say a player could not accept an award sponsored by a commercial concern. Inevitably, the rule was relaxed.

So I was enabled to accept the Texaco Award for 1974 and I was also fortunate enough to get the *Daily Express* Sportsman of the Year award. However, in many ways, what gave me most pleasure was that the Lions won the Team of the Year Award in the annual B.B.C. awards programme. Any honours I took were not so much personal awards as a striking tribute to what Ireland and the Lions had achieved in 1974.

I was amassing a collection of trophies in a hurry now, mementoes to remind me in the years ahead of my playing career. I had been awarded the M.B.E. for services to rugby in 1972, but I know better than anyone that rugby had rendered me better services than I could possibly give to this greatest of all games.

There were not many changes in the Irish side for the championship, Lynch and Moore's departures being the most notable. Lynch was replaced by Roger Clegg, while Willie Duggan, a good and abrasive number eight, took over from Moore.

The game against England saw the recall to out-half of Billy McCombe. He had won one cap in 1968 against France and now returned to the international scene after seven years. He is a magnificent place kicker and had shown tremendous form for Ulster in the inter-provincials and against the All Blacks. He played a major role in the defeat of England at Lansdowne Road. But Scotland beat us well in Murrayfield before we gave France a heavy beating in Dublin. That was to be my last international at Lansdowne Road and I suppose it was appropriate that I should have scored my only try for Ireland that afternoon. The back-slapping from the crowd after scoring was tougher for me than anything I had endured on the field, but it was a moment I shall always savour.

And so I come back to the game at the Arms Park, Ireland's last in 1975 and the final international of my career. I led a combined Ireland-Scotland team against England-Wales in a centenary match at the end of the season. As I left the pitch after the game, I was totally surprised to be captured by Eamonn Andrews to be the subject of his television programme, *This is Your Life*.

I was also delighted to help Ballymena to success in the Ulster Senior Cup; my contribution to the club down the years was of necessity severely restricted because of my representative commitments. Now free from the demands of Ulster and Ireland, I felt I could give something back to Ballymena to whom I owed so much. When I decided to retire and write that letter to Frank Humphreys, the secretary of the Ulster Branch, asking not to be considered for Ulster again, I did so with more than a touch of sadness, but I knew it was the right decision. I also knew that I still wanted to play for Ballymena; I owed the club my full attention for all it had given me through the years. I was extremely fortunate when I joined Ballymena. From the outset, I got nothing but help and encouragement. I owe a great debt to many people at Eaton Park, where the facilities are now as good as any in these islands. A visit to the ground is its testimony to the calibre of the men who run the club and who have been in charge down through the years. We had a humble Nissen hut as a pavilion in my early days, now the splendid clubhouse has just about every facility any player or member could ask for. Syd Millar and myself were paid a very special tribute when one of the rooms was named the Millar-McBride room.

My name is constantly being linked with that of Syd Millar and his influence on my career has been profound. He is however just one of many from the Ballymena club to whom I owe a debt of gratitude that can never adequately be repaid. I was lucky from the beginning to have as my second row partner

153

Hugh Allen, a greatly under-rated forward and better in my opinion than many who have been picked for Ireland. He was a great teacher to a raw recruit. Another who had much influence on me in the early days was former Irish international, Jonathan Moffett, capped twice for Ireland in 1961. He had enthusiasm for and understanding of the game and he went out of his way on many occasions to drive me to training sessions and matches. His was a generosity of spirit typical of the club.

Ballymena have had two great presidents in my playing period, the present incumbent, Bill Hanna, and his predecessor, Sam Anderson, who did so much to build the club into what it is today. The honorary secretary, Bob Leslie, is another whose contribution has been immense. Yet it seems wrong in many respects to mention some names and omit others, but it would be impossible to evaluate the work done by so many.

Now I am in a position to put something back into the club that gave me so much. I was delighted to help Ballymena to win the Ulster Senior League for the first time in 1976, the season after my retirement from representative rugby. I believe that one of the reasons we did not win the league outright in the past was due to the many calls on the club's players for representative games, which so often clashed with league fixtures. Those calls are still being made, and like the rest of the club, I rejoiced at the selection of three Ballymena players for Ireland's tour to New Zealand in May of 1976. Wallace McMaster, Harry Steele and Ian McIlrath are three great clubmen who will do credit to Ballymena and Ireland in New Zealand and I was especially pleased that both Ian and Harry won caps for Ireland in 1976; Wallace had achieved such a distinction for the first time in 1972 and has been a very good player for Ireland.

I intend to play on for Ballymena for at least one more season and then I hope to concentrate on the administrative side of the game, if I am needed there. I would like to do some coaching, notably among the younger players. Others have often asked if I had ambitions to be an Ulster and Irish selector. I do not think one can really plan to become a national or provincial selector. It may happen, but like so much on the playing side, it is an evolutionary process. I do not know, for instance, whether I have the qualities needed to make an international selector, but I do know that I could give something to young players.

My decision to stand down from the representative scene was a conscious one. Not the least of the benefits that I have gained is that I can now spend more time with Penny and my two children, Amanda and Paul. Often one hears reference to golf widows, who have to sit at home while their husbands hit the little pill around 18 holes. If ever there was a rugby widow, it was my wife Penny. The year after we were married, I was on tour with Ireland in Australia and five times in the intervening period, I have been away on tours overseas, quite apart from the constant demands at home. Not once has Penny complained. She was born into a rugby environment, but so were many others who often complain.

Penny has been a constant support to me. A few times when I felt I might decline offers to go on tour with Ireland and the Lions, it was Penny who urged me to go. I always went off absolutely secure in the knowledge that things at home would be more than adequately looked after.

There is a joke in our home when people ask us about the ages of our children, for the birth of both is always equated to my touring activities. Amanda, my daughter, is the elder of the two, she was born in March 1968, just over a month before I went to South Africa with the Lions, while Paul made his appearance in the world in August 1970 and that coincided with Ireland's tour to Argentina.

Those tours could not have been made by me were my employers, the Northern Bank, unwilling to give me the necessary leave. Through the years they have been extremely kind to me and I would like to acknowledge my gratitude here.

Mine has been an extremely fortunate life. I came from a happy home and my married life has been blessed with similar joys. I have known sadness on a personal level, primarily the death of my father when I was so young that I can only barely remember him; while a great sorrow later was the death of my brother, Tom, who drowned just before his 21st birthday. But there have been many good things to savour and I hope my children will enjoy the blessings and favours that have been bestowed on me.

Nevertheless, I worry at times about the society in which they are being brought up; not, I hasten to add, the immediate confines of their youth in Ballyclare, but the trend events have taken in Northern Ireland in the last six years. It would grieve me considerably if either of my children had to leave Ireland. This is their country; I want their future to be here in a peaceful society. I believe rugby has given a lead in terms of co-operation in this respect. The game in Ireland knows no political boundaries, no segregation. Of course there are many historical factors which have contributed to the problems that exist in Northern Ireland today, but what happened in the past should be left in the past, now the future must be the prime concern of us all. In this respect, I believe that education has a major part to play in breaking down barriers and killing the prejudices that have been nurtured by some in order to fulfil their own ends. I would like to see mixed education, and if and when it comes about, I believe a lot of the problems will disappear. If you divide at an early age, then divisions can at times grow wider. The local primary school I attended in Moneyglass was a mixed school; we took religious education separately, it is true, but it was above all a happy community. I believe tolerance to be a prime principle of Christianity and I firmly believe that sport moulds the character and teaches tolerance. It is a matter to give and take; you win a few and you lose a few. A staunch Protestant will go to Windsor Park and cheer himself hoarse for Ireland against another country. It will not worry him if some of the Irish players are Catholics. Yet how sad it is that when the games are over, religion will prove divisive. There is something radically wrong with that attitude. The saddest aspect of it is that for too long in

Northern Ireland people in high political places have encouraged the divisions.

When an Irish rugby team takes the field, it goes out representing Ireland—all Ireland. It will be made up of people from different walks of life and of different religious persuasions. That is as it should be. I remember being near the predominantly Protestant Shankill Road one evening shortly before going to South Africa with the Lions. As I walked to my car, a man cycling along the road stopped and said to me: 'Wally John, you're for South Africa. Then gud luck to ye'. The people from the Loyalist areas and the Catholic areas of Belfast, and other places in Northern Ireland, have always wished me luck when I was playing for Ireland and the Lions. As a North of Ireland Protestant, I can say that I have received nothing but kindness and consideration from the people in Dublin and all over Ireland. Indeed, I find it impossible to understand how people can stand on the terraces of a football field and acclaim a man one day and look on him as an enemy the next because he is of different religious or political persuasion.

Rugby has had a profound influence in moulding my character. It has taught me tolerance, and, I hope, the ability to win or lose with dignity, above all, to respect the other fellow. In this respect alone, sport has a vital role to play in man's relationship with man.

Many great things have happened in my life, but I can say without hesitation, that nothing has occurred of greater personal importance than that I was privileged to wear the green jersey of Ireland. May what it means, and what it stands for, and its glory never fade!

Index of Names